ENJOYING THE PREMIER LEAGUE RIDE 2019/2020

with Blade on a Bike

JAMES KEMP

WARNING: This book contains a few 'naughty' words along the way. Proceed with caution :)

First published in Great Britain in 2020 by
Bannister Publications Ltd
118 Saltergate, Chesterfield, Derbyshire S40 1NG

ISBN: 978-1-909813-70-0

Cover illustration by Luke Prest © www.lukeprest.com
Typeset in GFY Palmer W00

Printed and bound in Great Britain

This book was self-published by Bannister Publications.
For more information on self-publishing visit:

www.bannisterpublications.com

About This Book

All profits from the sale of this book will go to
The Sheffield's Children's Hospital

A word from the Author

I hope by sharing with you all my emotions on this incredible journey it may help in some way.

I don't mind sharing that I have struggled with Mental Health issues for the past 5 years. There is no one fix and most live with it all their lives. We are all different but I have learnt that talking about issues is better than not.

I hope that even non football fans (I hear they exist) will find this helpful.

"The efforts of James should be commended, particularly with the added hurdle of Covid-19 to contend with as he made his way around the country in our first season back in the Premier League. Hopefully this book will give fellow Blades supporters an insight into what he went through on the path to raising vital funds for an organisation that is close to the hearts of everyone associated with our great city. It is heart-warming to learn of fans of our club supporting the community positively and James certainly fits into that category."

- Chris Wilder

Foreword by Alan Biggs

When they talk about so-called "ordinary" people doing "extraordinary" things there is no finer example than James Kemp. Except there's nothing exactly ordinary about James. You couldn't do what he's done, certainly neither could I!

As someone who pats himself on the back for running the odd half marathon now and then, it's hard to comprehend the scale of the challenge James took on. The numbers are elsewhere. And yet the bottom line for him is the amount he raised for Sheffield Children's Hospital.

The second number is greater than the first in being closer to everyone's heart, not least the man himself. But the physical effort involved was clearly phenomenal.

And what about the planning? When to set off? Overnight stays and how many? Road closures? Weather?

James is a modest chap, almost matter of fact about it all in conversation - as I discovered when he guested on my Sheffield Live TV show in January, 2020.

But he's accumulated some fantastic stories along the way, including heart-warming tales of the reception he received from rival football fans in far-flung places.

That was in the first two-thirds of the season, of course. The remainder of it must have been purgatory - slogging to places like Southampton and not even being able to watch a game at the end of it.

Yet James pedalled determinedly on, completing the challenge he talked himself into when he was assessing the chances of his beloved Blades making it to the Premier League.

To the best of my knowledge he didn't discuss their prospects of getting into Europe or he'd have been sweating even more profusely on his saddle!

As we all know, Chris Wilder's side came mighty close on that front as well. But James himself certainly got into Europe and came out well beyond the other side when you tot up his incredible mileage.

Very well done, sir. I'm certain this will be as entertaining a read as the journey must have been excruciating. And you have done your club and city proud.

Introduction

Me and my big mouth 4 years ago. The opening day of the season in League One, our 5th consecutive season in the 'pub league' saw us travel to Gillingham. My son, Tom, Cheese and I set off for the long trip full of optimism as Nigel Adkins had been appointed Manager. We were all saying this is it, the season we finally leave this god forsaken League. It was scorching, it usually is on the opening day of the season. As we sat/stood on the temporary scaffold stand (that's been in place for years), our mood got lower with every minute. Well, when we left The Priestfield Stadium it was 3-0 to the Gills. It ended 4-0. The optimism had gone in less than 60 minutes. On the long journey home I said to myself 'if we ever make it to the top flight I will cycle to all away games. I was safe with that thought, wasn't I?'

I got back home and went into my local where I was greeted with some sniggers and some sympathy.

For the first time in my life I honestly thought we would never make it back to the Premier League, the gap was, in my mind, immense. Too wide to be bridged. That season we finished 11th. 11th for goodness sake!

For some reason Nigel Adkins sent the players out after the last match to thank the fans. We had all long since gone home. We certainly weren't United. It seemed Nigel Adkins was going to be given another crack at it but all of a sudden he was gone and Chris Wilder was appointed. There was the usual 'what's he done at this level' comments but like all the others before I was willing him to succeed.

After a pretty average start, which saw us bottom of the league after 3 games, the season turned with a trip to the off licence, not for me but for the team. Since that day at Millwall we simply haven't looked back. Reaching 100 points was just not, even in the most positive of Blades minds possible. The Championship was ours and ok it was the third tier but 30,000 plus Blades at the Lane for the final game against Chesterfield we're loving every minute.

The promotion party at Kevin Gages Manor House was as you'd expect was rather boisterous. I was on a flight at 7am the following morning to Portugal so the intention was to take it easy. I set my alarm for 6pm when I would stop drinking and go home. That didn't work out and at 12.30am got to bed. How I got up at 3am to get to the airport is a question I still get asked to this day. So funny in the Taxi on the way home, I was asking the driver if he knew Jack O'Connell. He said 'No, who is he?' I replied by telling him he's magic and wears a magic hat. Also if you throw a brick at him he would head the fucker back. The 4 of us in the Taxi were pissing ourselves.

Still not really thinking about my promise 18 months previous as the 'Championship' was a different level altogether, well that's what our neighbours in South Barnsley kept telling us.

Fast forward to May 2019 and me as Scooby Doo at Stoke started thinking 'how on earth do I deliver the promise I made only 3 1/2 years previous.'

The first concern was would I be able to get tickets?

I have enough loyalty points for when we are allocated 3,000 but may struggle at the smaller grounds.

When the fixtures came out in June we all knew we would be away for the first match as United had requested this to allow more time to complete works to Bramall Lane to comply with Premier League rules. Bournemouth! Really? Nothing like being eased in gently.

I had said after raising for different charities I wouldn't do it again as people do get apathetic when another message pops up on Social Media, however I have always wanted to raise money for The Children's Hospital.

So the planning commenced.

Total Miles: 3000
Total Ascent: 130,000ft
www.justgiving.com/fundraising/james-kemp1889

CHAPTER 1

Bournemouth, 10th August

Early morning at the Lane secured me a ticket and just as early set off on the Thursday prior to the game. Hotels booked along the way I knew exactly how many miles I had each day.

Day 1 was 84 miles to Southam. Weather was kind and made good progress. In fact I arrived at 2pm. The weather took a turn for the worst on Day 2. The wind got stronger and I got drenched towards the end of the ride. Although the first two days were comfortable and without incident I was concerned I had left myself too many miles on the day of the match, 64. Also the forecast was for 60mph head winds. With this in mind I went to bed early. The Friday night locals in Hungerford obviously didn't care I needed sleep and kept me awake till late. After a restless night I woke at 5. Adrenaline keeping me going, I got going at just after 6am.

OOF!

PARKING FOR
VISITORS TO
CEMETERY

P Mon - Fri
9 am - 5 pm
1 hour
No return
within 1 hour

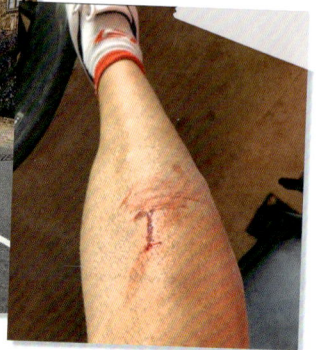

After an hour I was concerned that my average speed was under 10mph due to my heavy load and strong wind. Thankfully I sped up and made it to Bournemouth for midday. Wanting a picture (as proof) I asked a guy who was walking past to take my picture. When he turned round I was surprised to see it was 'O Lord' Michael Brown. I had lots of interest from both sets of fans and was interviewed by John Shires of Calendar. As the Vitality is a little way from the centre of Bournemouth, I entered the ground when the turnstiles opened at 1.30. It wasn't long until my brother, Simon and his friend Oz arrived. After a couple of beers I seriously felt drunk. Kick off, this is it, we're in the big time again.

Even when Bournemouth scored I wasn't despondent as the performance was excellent. Then, shortly after Billy Sharp had come off the bench, we were awarded a free kick deep in Bournemouth's half. The ball was passed down the right then quickly crossed in by Baldy. I couldn't make out what was happening, there were legs flying everywhere. Then all of a sudden the guy next to me was kissing me and we went bonkers. All football fans who have followed their team through highs and in our case, lows, knows that feeling of elation when a goal goes in late on. Once things had settled down the guy in front pointed out that there was blood all over my leg. Eh? How did that happen? No issues cycling 240 miles but Billy scores and....... What an opener.

CHERRIES 1-1 BLADES

Billy Sharp celebrates with the Blades fans at Bournemouth

Power of the people makes all the difference

It was fitting that Billy Sharp, one of the driving forces behind Sheffield United's climb from the third tier to the top-flight, scored the goal which ensured the Blades claimed the point their efforts deserved.

The centre-forward's goal, with only two minutes of normal time remaining, sparked exuberant celebrations in the away end and the technical area too.

Having fallen behind midway through the second-half, when Chris Mepham prodded Bournemouth in front, Wilder made no apology for United's reaction.

"That at the end, people can think: 'Is this an over celebration?'

"No. It's just the enjoyment of a good job," he said. "They've got a great connection. These boys are really down to earth and honest,

and they've earned the right to play in the Premier League."

David McGoldrick had twice gone close for United following John Lundstram assists. Callum Robinson also forced a save from Aaron Ramsdale.

But United, who improved as the afternoon wore on, were rewarded for their persistence when Sharp, the most prolific marksman in the English game this century, converted for the first time at the highest level.

Fellow substitute Oli McBurnie, one of three United debutants, had seen a shot blocked in the earlier melee.

"We had to do amazing things to get here," Wilder said. "We don't want it to just pass us by."

TEAMS

AFC BOURNEMOUTH: Ramsdale, Cook, Ake, King, Lerma, Rico, Mepham, Billing, Smith, Wilson (Solanke 89), Fraser. Not used: Boruc, Surman, Ibe, Daniels, Wilson, Simpson.

SHEFFIELD UNITED: Henderson, Stevens, Baldock, Basham (Sharp 81), Egan, O'Connell, Norwood, Fleck, Lundstram (L Freeman 78), McGoldrick (McBurnie 63), Robinson. Not used: Moore, Jagielka, Osborn, Besic.

REFEREE: Kevin Friend (Leicestershire).

STATS

CHERRIES		BLADES
53	POSS %	47
13	SHOTS	8
3	SHOTS ON TARGET	3
3	CORNERS	4
10	FOULS	19

THE PROOF THAT SHARP CAN CUT IT

JAMES SHIELD
The Star's Blades writer

Email: james.shield@jpimedia.co.uk
Twitter: @JamesShield1

Billy Sharp has spent the summer watching, reading and patiently waiting for the moment when he could prove a very important point.

That it arrived and was seized during Sheffield United's first match of the Premier League campaign served as a reminder to those who have been belittling his talents that the centre-forward – the highest scoring player in English football this century – can pose the same type of threat to top-flight defences as those in the Championship.

Over the summer focus has shifted onto the £40 million of talent United have brought to the Lane.

How, for example, would Oli McBurnie perform after becoming the club's record transfer signing?

Could Callum Robinson – or, longer term, Lys Mousset – forge an effective partnership with the former Swansea City striker?

Sharp, now aged 33 and supposedly in the autumn of his career, barely got a mention.

There is no room for sentiment, plenty of self-appointed experts told us, at elite level.

What they forgot,

however, is that Sharp is as adept at changing narratives as he is claiming goals.

For each of the past two years, he has been forced to listen to people tell him he is now too old or too slow to be the difference-maker.

And every single time, the critics have been forced to eat their words.

Manager Chris Wilder acknowledged following Saturday's contest – which Sharp ensured ended in a 1-1 draw – that likes of McBurnie and Robinson represent the future for United. Time, being 23 and 24 respectively, is on their side.

But as Sharp's effort two minutes from the end of normal time demonstrated, after Chris Mepham had earlier given Eddie Howe's team the lead, Sharp remains the most clinical finisher at the manager's disposal. Fact. End of argument.

The strike ensured United's persistence and discipline did not go unrewarded. And proved speed of thought can be even more effective than speed of foot in rarefied company.

As the ball bounced around in the penalty box, Bournemouth's defence trying and failing to clear George Baldock's cross, it was Sharp who reacted first when his

Billy Sharp applauds the fans at the end of the game

fellow substitute McBurnie saw an effort blocked seconds earlier.

Having drifted into position and adjusting his body shape in anticipation of something falling his way, Sharp reacted quicker than anyone, prodding home from point blank range before sprinting towards the away supporters.

A lifelong United fan himself, their captain, leader and already a legend wanted to

celebrate his first goal on the greatest domestic stage of all with them. His people.

"He tries to steal my thunder all the time," Wilder joked afterwards.

"Mr Sheffield United isn't he. Well, do you know what, I'll gladly let him steal it today."

"He scores goals doesn't he," Howe commented afterwards.

He does. And will continue to do so.

David McGoldrick, Oliver McBurnie and Luke Freeman celebrate

Sharp scrambles home his first Premiership goal

Enda Stevens fights for possession

PLAYER RATINGS

DEAN HENDERSON — 8
Made a stunning save to deny Billing.

GEORGE BALDOCK — 8
A bundle of energy down the right. Helped create leveller.

CHRIS BASHAM — 7
A little more reserved than the swashbuckling Basham.

JOHN EGAN — 8
Very good. In the right place at the right time.

JACK O'CONNELL — 8
Looked to get forward down the left.

ENDA STEVENS — 8
His driving runs helped United transition quickly.

JOHN FLECK — 7
A quiet start but grew into the game.

OLIVER NORWOOD — 8
Excellent set piece delivery and showed bite in his tackles.

CALLUM ROBINSON — 7
Full of running throughout the game.

DAVID MCGOLDRICK — 7
Twice went close and dropped deep to link up play.

MAN OF THE MATCH

JOHN LUNDSTRAM — 8
Could have had a hat-trick of assists after playing in McGoldrick (twice) and Robinson.

SUBSTITUTES

OLIVER MCBURNIE — 7
Bright debut. Dropped deep to pick up possession and wasn't scared to run at defenders.

LUKE FREEMAN — 7
Showed a few glimpses of his ability.

BILLY SHARP — 8
Does what Billy Sharp does. The EFL's highest goalscorer of the 21st century is finally off the mark in the Premier League.

HIGHLIGHT

Billy Sharp's late equaliser ensured Sheffield United celebrated their return to the Premier League with a point.

After being introduced as a substitute, Sharp prodded the home with only two minutes of normal time remaining, sparking wonderful scenes both on the pitch and in the stand where he raced to celebrate with the travelling support.

It was also a deeply personal moment, with Sharp scoring his first ever goal in the competition for the club he has followed since childhood. And a reminder Sharp has no intention of being content with a peripheral role this term.

LOWLIGHT

Clean sheets will be difficult for United to come by this term, given the array of attacking talent they will face.

Bournemouth, for example, selected England international Callum Wilson and Joshua King, capped 40 times by Norway, up front on Saturday afternoon. So in a sense, Mepham's effort was not the lowlight. Instead, that came midway through the opening period when, having missed a chance to take an early lead through David McGoldrick, the Blades struggled to retain possession and were hustled into mistakes by the strength of the opposition's 'press'.

CHAPTER 2

Chelsea, 31st August

A great opening home win against Crystal Palace meant my voice would not return for a few more days. The following week against Leicester saw us lose our first match but we certainly weren't disgraced.

For some crazy reason I thought it would be a great idea to allow just Friday and Saturday morning for the Chelsea trip. Luckily Wayne, an old school pal, had a ticket and offered to do back up which at least meant I would be pannier free. In the 3 weeks since the trip to Bournemouth the weather had been still with no wind whatsoever. It had to return and of course it had to be on the Friday I set off. A 7.15 set off saw me make good progress and my first meet with Wayne after 30 miles arrived in little time. A nice stop in a small village for a sandwich was welcome and a bonus promise from the owner that she would sponsor me. Wayne, once a

salesman always a salesman.
I've never thought of
Leicestershire as a hilly county
but when the wind is against
doing 113 miles the mounds
all felt like Winnets Pass!
I stayed in a farm house near
Olney, lovely place, shame
my stay would be so brief.
My legs were in a reight
tangle during the night
which meant little sleep.
Knowing I'd stupidly left far
too many miles to do I set
off at 6.30 on the Saturday.
My ass was a tad tender.
I was going well until my
left calf decided to start
giving me some jip.
The pain got quite bad to
the point where I was cycling
with just my right leg.
Wayne sorted the drugs
which took the edge off.
The route into London
worked out well and I was
soon heading through Earls
Court where adrenaline

started kicking in, helped by a few hundred Blades outside a few pubs cheering me on. I heard someone shout 'go on James' it was Toms mate, Cheese. After I had a photo at the ground I then cycled to where Wayne had parked. I stopped at some lights and noticed I was outside what looked like Chelsea's main pub. A few giants of men shouted 'you ain't fackin cycled ere as yer?' I replied telling them my plan to do all away matches and their response was to invite me in for a beer! It was recommended I take my shirt off which I didn't debate. Quality set of blokes.

On the Friday Anna & Jordan managed to get hold of tickets so drove down early. Met up with Cousin Sam and

Reverend Steve Mabey

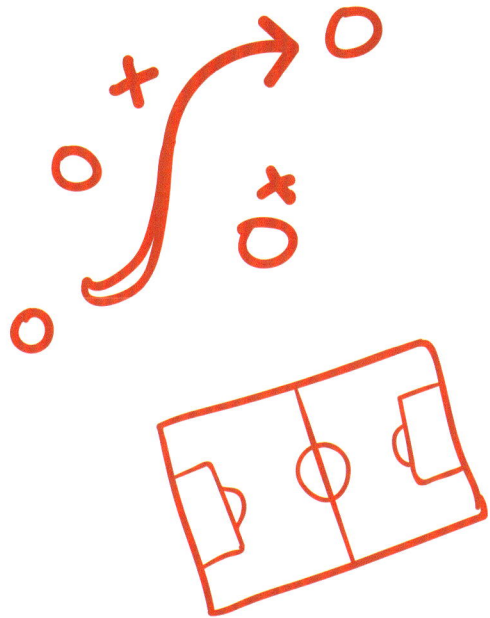

Guy, an old work contact.
Once in the ground, for the first time it felt proper Premier League. The noise from the Blades was incredible, even after going 2-0 down. At half time we discussed whether to leave for a beer if it got to 4-0. As expected, that was soon forgotten after only a minute into the second half when Robinson finished off a great Enda move down the left. 30 minutes previous me and a few guys around me were saying 'he ain't good enough' now he's our hero! The fickle football fan in all our glory. Could we? Nah chance, not at Chelsea. I never thought the scenes at Bournemouth could be repeated but when the 2nd goal went in we went crazy. Hugging and kissing complete strangers is not my usual behaviour but it's becoming a regular occurrence. Unreal! Just unreal. I genuinely feel the fans have given the opposition too much respect. as well as the players in some instances. Chris Wilder is excellent at removing that. Whatever the future holds our current manager is now the best we've ever had in my lifetime. Yes there is a team behind him but every successful group needs a true leader whose troops would do anything for.

CHELSEA 2 BLADES 2

JAMES WILSON/SPORTIMAGE

Chris Wilder and Lys Mousset embrace at the final whistle

Wilder's pang of regret over poor defending

What had threatened to become a lesson in the importance of small details became one in the art of never giving up instead.

Two goals down to the five-time Premier League champions and by their manager's own admission looking a pretty awe-struck bunch, Sheffield United were in danger of suffering a beating by Chelsea following a careless first-half performance. But Callum Robinson's strike immediately after the interval changed the course of the game. To such an extent that, by the time Lys Mousset glanced the ball beyond Kepa Arrizabalaga, even Frank Lampard refused to try and pretend the visitors were not worthy of their point.

It spoke volumes about both his team's Premier

TEAMS

Chelsea: Kepa; Azpilicueta, Zouma, Tomori, Emerson; Jorginho, Kovacic (Batshuayi 83); Pulisic, Barkley (Willian 60), Mount; Abraham (Gilmour 84). Subs: Caballero, Christensen, Alonso, Giroud.
Blades: Henderson; Baldock, Basham (Osborn 84), Egan, O'Connell, Stevens; Norwood, Lundstram, L. Freeman (Mousset 79); McBurnie (McGoldrick 63); Robinson. Subs: Moore, Sharp, Stearman, Besic.

Referee: Stuart Attwell
Attendance: 40,560

League potential and the standards they have set, that Chris Wilder departed Stamford Bridge with a pang of regret. Had they taken care of business at the back, he ventured during the post-match briefing, United might well have secured an even more eye-catching result.

"I thought we deserved it," Wilder said. "But I was disappointed with their goals. We could have done better on both. Take nothing away from the boys. How can you? Still, we know we should have kept them out. We stood off them a bit and then gave some silly things away. But the boys, all of them, dug in and dug it out. And that's what being at this level is all about."

STATS

BLUES		BLADES
62	POSS %	38
13	SHOTS	8
5	SHOTS ON TARGET	2
3	CORNERS	4
6	FOULS	11

BLADES ARE LOOKING THE REAL DEAL

JAMES SHIELD
The Star's Blades writer

Email: james.shield@jpimedia.co.uk
Twitter: @JamesShield1

So driven are Sheffield United, so convinced is Chris Wilder about the potential of this team, you get the impression he is more concerned about the seven point gap between themselves and early leaders Liverpool than the two which separate his players from the relegation places.

At the beginning of the season, Wilder's insistence that survival did not represent the extent of their ambition was dismissed as rhetoric. Bombastic nonsense from a manager who had forgotten how to lose. But four weeks in, and following a battling draw with Chelsea, people might have to revise their opinions. Because, rather than simply appearing glad to be there, United look like they belong at the highest level.

Saturday's match at Stamford Bridge was instructive for a whole host of reasons. It could, if one of Wilder's post-game messages resonated inside the away dressing room, be hugely significant too. "Sometimes, I think the coaching staff believe in the players a little bit more than they believe in themselves," he said. "I'm not bothered

about reputations or the names on the back of shirts. We are here to be competitive. We are here to show that we are deserving of our place. I don't want us to come away from anywhere, even if we do get undone, wondering about what might have been."

Wilder was referring, of course, to the subdued first-half performance United produced in west London. For the first time since being promoted from the Championship, they appeared in awe of their opponents. It was understandable. After drawing with AFC Bournemouth, beating Crystal Palace and then losing a tight encounter with Leicester City, the trip to SW6 was a proper welcome back to the big time for a club which, as Wilder later reminded, was plying its trade in the third tier only three years ago.

To begin with, despite his claims to the contrary, they did not handle it well. Tammy Abraham, Chelsea's preciously talented centre-forward, had already engineered several promising situations before twice taking advantage of defensive errors. But when Callum Robinson reduced the deficit early in the second period, profiting from some good work by the excellent

Enda Stevens, they gained a renewed sense of purpose. Abraham went close again, forcing an excellent save from Dean Henderson, and Ross Barkley also tested his handling. But by the time Lys Mousset equalised, with Robinson providing the assist, the momentum had swung decisively in United's favour.

The Frenchman - a fearsome combination of raw power, pace and skill - seems destined to become

an invaluable asset over the course of the campaign.

"Three years ago, we were bottom of League One," Wilder continued. "Now, we are going toe to toe with former Premier League champions.

"I don't want us to stand off the opposition. I want us to go out there and play our game. We deserve to be here, I told the lads (during the interval) 'this isn't a cup tie.' We are here on merit."

Callum Robinson (centre) celebrates scoring the Blades first goal

JAMES WILSON/SPORTIMAGE

Blades score their second goal of the game with a deflected effort from Lys Mousset

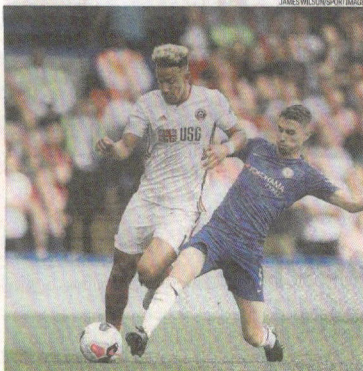

JAMES WILSON/SPORTIMAGE

Callum Robinson battles Chelsea's Jorginho for the ball

JAMES WILSON/SPORTIMAGE

Lys Mousset, centre, celebrates scoring the Blades equaliser

HIGHLIGHT

Sheffield United's second goal might have been slightly fortuitous. But they deserved their slice of luck.

Two-nil down at half-time, United showed huge amounts of courage and no little skill to force themselves back on level terms against a team which, despite not being the force of old, still possesses players of world class calibre.

The momentum was in United's favour when they equalised.

LOWLIGHT

Chelsea were the better team before the break by some margin. But both of Tammy Abraham's goals were preventable.

When the dust settles on the game, and with some tough tests to come, United must show greater attention to detail when the opposition is on top.

Otherwise, in future, they might not be able to plot a course back into the game.

PLAYER RATINGS

DEAN HENDERSON — 7
His superb save prevented Chelsea scoring a third

GEORGE BALDOCK — 7
Showed a high level of passion throughout

CHRIS BASHAM — 7
Almost set up equaliser for Robinson with superb cross

JOHN EGAN — 7
Rare mistake for second goal but read game superbly

JACK O'CONNELL — 7
Got tangled up with Egan a bit but also did plenty right

ENDA STEVENS — 9
Set up Robinson's equaliser superbly. Belongs at this level

OLIVER NORWOOD — 7
Pinged the ball about with aplomb and did the ugly stuff

JOHN LUNDSTRAM — 8
Good in the first half, excellent second half

LUKE FREEMAN — 7
Superb late challenge on Jorginho, flashes of quality

CALLUM ROBINSON — 9
A goal, an assist, and ran his blood to water

OLI MCBURNIE — 6
Failed to grasp his chance and picked up a booking

SUBSTITUTES

DAVID MCGOLDRICK — 7
Showed some neat touches when he dropped deep

LYS MOUSSET — 8
Equaliser might go down as an own goal but he deserves it for his contribution

BEN OSBORN — 6
Had a good chance to level

England v Bulgaria, 7th August

One of my best mates, Ashley was 50 earlier in the year and I wanted to show my appreciation for him being there when my chips were very down.

It was my first full international game and to be honest I felt the whole experience was dull. No atmosphere, lack of excitement on the pitch and no passion in the stands. Maybe if it were Scotland or Germany it would have been different. One thing that did really please me was how well received we were as Blades. Every fan really pleased for us.

CHAPTER 3

Everton, 21st September

I think most Blades were a bit flat after losing to Southampton as we deserved at least a point and it was a game we 'targeted' as one we should be looking to get maximum points from, well by the fans anyway.

Late September brought lovely weather. Only a short one, ish anyway, compared to the opening two.
My cousin, Martin only lives 20 miles from Liverpool so it was a nice, albeit hilly ride across the Peaks. I learnt a harsh lesson from the opening two matches, not to leave myself too much to do on the day of the match. It was nice to take my time, especially as the weather was perfect. Rather than dwell on the inevitable cold weather to come over the coming months I lapped up the here and now. Arriving at Martins in good time it was nice to catch up. Top man and top family. Martin and I went out but I was strong not to have

a beer, until we got back that is.. Slept very well and didn't need to set off till 11. Wasn't long till I was 7 miles away from Goodison. Saw a group of Blades outside a pub so thought it was time to stick my red and white stripes on. I had my own song 'Blade on a bike' from the guys. Alan Pickard (who runs coaches) since told me it was he who offered me a pint through the fence. Would have loved one but didn't want to fail this close to the ground. For anyone who has done any endurance event they will get how much any amount of encouragement gives you. I was soon at Goodison and greeted by some really nice people. To date all 3 clubs have been brilliant and welcoming. The match started in brilliant sunshine. The Blades looked like the weather was getting to them as Everton were dominant. Just prior to half time we had a corner. I had a sneaky feeling so started videoing it. The ball ended up in the net but, probably because of what happened the week before, we

Baking hot at Goodison

Everton v Sheffield Utd (15:00BST)

Gary Rose
BBC Sport at Goodison Park

BBC

It is baking hot at Goodison today and no surprises to see business booming at The Winslow Hotel outside the ground.

I bumped into a chap who is gasping for a liquid refreshment, a well deserved one too.

Sheffield United fan James Kemp is cycling to every away game this season to raise money for Sheffield Children's Home and has just knocked off the 80+ miles from Sheffield to Everton.

"This is one of the easier ones," James says. "It is Brighton before Christmas I'm not looking forward to!"

didn't really know whether to celebrate or not. Anyway the VAR ruled in our favour and remarkably we were one up. The second half was marginally better and when Lundstrum put the Moose through to score the 2nd there was no doubt and the usual hugging complete strangers commenced! It was brilliant to enjoy the last 10 minutes knowing we had won. It was great to see Jags get an excellent welcome from the Toffees fans.

After the final whistle I blasted the 3 miles to Lime Street station to get an earlier train, which was delayed. On this journey I'm meeting a new group of football fans. The ones that travel by train. Most alone but all great guys. Really enjoying meeting different clubs fans. On the train there were obviously loads of Blades but also Everton fans, Bolton, Man City and Sunderland. All, without exception, well-behaved normal people. When I arrived earlier at Goodison Park a guy who said he was a freelance BBC reporter asked if he could interview me. I didn't think anything of it until a couple of days later my nephew sent me a message saying that I was on the BBC Football Instagram page. I haven't a clue how to use Instagram but the article received nearly 10,000 likes and numerous great comments.

21

TOFFEES 0 BLADES 2

John Lundstram of Sheffield United turns Bernard of Everton

Victory gives Lundstram the last laugh

An international manager spent Saturday evening reflecting on a terrible misjudgement.

Roberto Martinez, now head coach of Belgium and previously Everton's manager, was the person responsible for telling John Lundstram he did not possess the calibre to progress at Goodison Park.

Four years later, after Marco Silva's predecessor effectively engineered his exit, the Sheffield United midfielder exacted revenge in the most devastating fashion.

Lundstram's pass, which presented Lys Mousset with the chance to seal a famous victory following Yerry Mina's own goal, exposed Martinez's error in glorious technicolour.

Not only because of its execution – both the

TEAMS

Everton: Pickford, Keane, Richarlison, Delph, Sigurdsson, Digne, Mina, Schneiderlin (Iwobi 55), Bernard (Tosun 55), Coleman, Kean. Not used: Stekelenburg, Holgate, Calvert-Lewin, Walcott, Davies.
Sheffield United: Henderson, Basham, Egan, O'Connell, Stevens, Baldock, Norwood (Jagielka 62), Fleck, Lundstram, McBurnie (Osborn 83), Robinson (Mousset 62). Not used: Moore, L Freeman, Morrison, K Freeman.
Attendance: 39,354
Referee: Simon Hooper (Wiltshire).

trajectory and weight were absolutely perfect – but also the intellect behind it.

Surging forward on the counter, as the hosts pressed for an equaliser, Lundstram required little more than a second to identify the possibilities unfolding in front of him. Mousset's strike – officially his first since joining United earlier this summer – ensured Wilders's side finished the contest comfortably ahead of the point per game average which usually guarantees survival.

But their success was built at the back where, as Everton dominated possession throughout the first-half, Jack O'Connell, Chris Basham and John Egan in particular produced defensive masterclasses.

STATS

TOFFEES		BLADES
70	POSS %	30
16	SHOTS	2
3	SHOTS ON TARGET	1
12	CORNERS	3
0	FOULS	9

TRUE GRIT HAS BLADES ON A HIGH

JAMES SHIELD
The Star's Blades writer

Email: james.shield@jpimedia.co.uk
Twitter: @JamesShield1

Football, is it fair to say, has become obsessed with science.

Whereas managers only used to be bothered about the final scoreline, now they fuss over things like possession percentages, metres run and other statistics. It is a trend which means things impossible to quantify are no longer viewed as important. But here is the rub. Qualities like personality, commitment and strength of character are what usually decide the outcome of matches.

Saturday's fixture at Goodison Park supported this argument. Everton saw more of the ball and enjoyed more shots on target. But Sheffield United prevailed because they were prepared to dig-in and, during a one-sided first-half, roll with the punches.

"I just thought we turned the ball over too much," Chris Wilder said afterwards. "We've set high standards over the last three years. It's a funny old game because last week (against Southampton) I thought we were excellent and lost. I'm not going to con the punters by saying we were brilliant here. I thought we were under the cosh for the majority of it."

Although Wilder's analysis was overly critical – deliberately so to guard against complacency – United did appear destined to ensure a difficult afternoon when Marco Silva's players seized control of the opening exchanges. The trouble was, from the Portuguese's perspective, the opposition's durability gnawed away at their confidence. Dominant at the start, Everton finished the contest looking disillusioned, lost and totally bereft of ideas. United, by contrast, maintained their sense of purpose.

Although Lys Mousset's goal sealed United's victory, Yerry Mina having earlier turned into his own net, this success was secured at the back. As Richarlison threatened to run riot, dragging United's midfielders out of position by drifting effortlessly across the pitch, Chris Basham and Jack O'Connell, marshalled by the excellent John Egan, combined to produce a defensive masterclass. It wasn't always pretty. But that was the point. Wilder's men were prepared to go the extra mile and, as Basham reminded when he flung himself in front of one of the Brazilian's passes, do whatever it took to prevail.

"Half our team are Scousers," Wilder said. "So it was a big day for them. I didn't realise all of them were Liverpool fans. I thought John

Lundstram supported Everton."

"Joking aside," he continued. "I know all about rivalries. Sheffield United and Sheffield Wednesday, I know what that means because I'm a Blade. So did that play a part. I honestly don't know. But what I do is that they'll have been determined to go out there and give absolutely everything. The same, to be honest, as they always do."

It would be a mistake, however, to attribute United's success to guts and grit alone. Their opener – Callum Robinson and O'Connell unnerving Jordan Pickford before Mina connected with Oliver Norwood's corner – might have been a shade fortuitous. But there were examples of real technical excellence and tactical sophistication too.

Lundstram's pass, which presented Mousset with the chance to slide home past Pickford, was simply superb.

John Lundstram set up United's second goal

SPORTIMAGE

Lys Mousset celebrates opening his account with the Blades

Mina scores an own goal to put the Blades in front

Dean Henderson waves to the travelling United fans

PLAYER RATINGS

HENDERSON
8
Made a smart save to deny Kean when the youngster enjoyed a rare sight of goal. Booked early

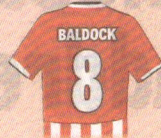

BALDOCK
8
Dealt well with lively Bernard down the left even if tempers did boil over in the corner after one challenge

BASHAM
8
Barely left Bernard alone all afternoon. Shifted into midfield for last half an hour or so after Norwood went off

EGAN
9
A rock all afternoon, keeping Everton's lively forwards at bay and denied Kean with a superb block later in the game

O'CONNELL
8
Another colossal display alongside his fellow defenders to keep a deserved clean sheet. Linked up with Stevens well

STEVENS
8
A couple more nutmegs to add to the growing collection and another impressive display, as well.

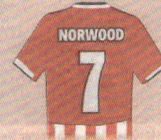

NORWOOD
7
Picked up an early booking which saw him walking a tight-rope for the rest of the game. Taken off.

LUNDSTRAM
8
On his return to Goodison Park the midfielder shone with an energetic display, capped with a superb assist

FLECK
7
A combative display from the Scot in midfield who put his foot in to great effect when it was needed

MCBURNIE
7
Ran his blood to water for the cause once again and did well on the scraps of play he picked up.

ROBINSON
6
Couldn't get in the game with a lack of service and was berated by Lundstram after failing to get onto a pass.

SUBSTITUTES

LYS MOUSSET 3
Excellent cameo, capped by a calm finish for the second goal

PHIL JAGIELKA 7
A calming influence for the back four

BEN OSBORN N/A
Came on late on to shore up midfield and see out the points

HIGHLIGHT

John Lundstram's pass, which provided the assist for Lys Mousset's goal, was superb. If a player from one of the top six clubs had produced it, rather than one who had effectively been declared surplus to requirements by the team he was competing against, people would have be eulogising about it for days to come. Sliding the ball into space, showing an awareness of the situation which could unfold if he executed it properly, Lundstram demonstrated there is more to his game than simply power and industry. The former Everton and Oxford midfielder has been a fixture in their preferred Premier League line-up.

LOWLIGHT

Everton manager Marco Silva questioned if United's first goal should have been awarded after VAR officials decided Callum Robinson and Jack O'Connell had not impeded Jordan Pickford before Yerry Mina turned Oliver Norwood's corner into his own net. The Portuguese would have been better asking if Pickford had done enough to prevent the ball from striking his centre-half in the first place. If there really is a doubt about whether or not it should have stood, the game is in a very bad place indeed. In fact, it is probably in danger of becoming a non-contact sport as replays showed the goalkeeper simply had not been strong enough under a fair but robust challenge.

CHAPTER 4

Watford, 5th October

Last weeks narrow defeat to Liverpool, the European Champions, was a fantastic effort and gave all Blades many reasons to be optimistic.

The past few days had brought a considerable amount of rain but thankfully today (Thursday) was dry, albeit a lot cooler (5 degrees). So, although I kept with the bib shorts, the new coat came out. After dropping Lola off at Doggy Hotel I set off. I felt strong for the morning and the first 38 miles went quickly. Then, I came across something I've never faced before. Just before Castle Donnington the route took me on a trail. I had no choice as the road joined the A50. As I got a mile down the trail I came close to the River Trent. When I say close I mean about 100 yards away but that's where I met the water. The kid in me kept me cycling until the water came over half way up my wheels. Slight panic, thinking about the bearings I got off and carried the bike above my head, the water literally above my waist.

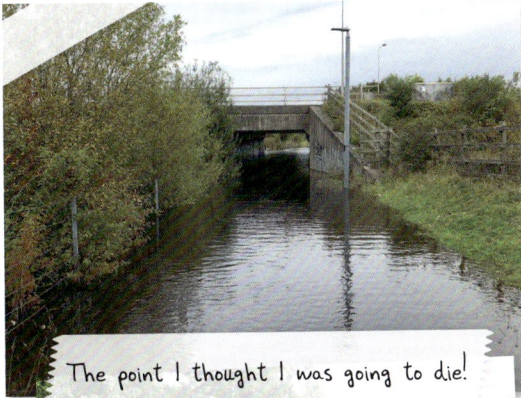

The point I thought I was going to die!

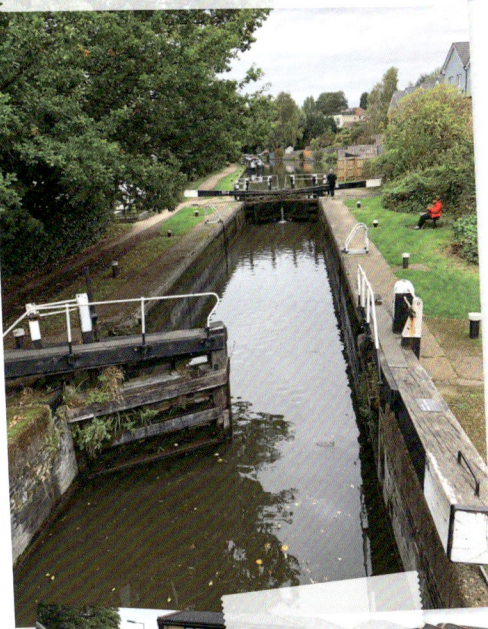

I actually thought I'm going to die here and miss the bloody match! Eventually got through and was very thankful I'd chosen to wear the bib shorts. My feet were soaked and cold. No worries I thought, next cafe after Castle Donnington I'd stop and dry out. Yeah right, believe it or not I didn't come across a pub or cafe for another 20 miles. Eventually found a magic country pub and was so tempted to order a pint but with 30 miles left thought better of it. Eventually arrived at South Kilworth, nice B&B (The Hollies) next door to a pub. After I dried out I met the owner, Tim. The usual question followed 'where you cycled from?' Sheffield I replied. 'No way! I'm from Sheffield.' Now most Football fans from Cities with more than one club will relate to this. I looked him in the eye, he looked me in the eye, almost like an old Western dual. 'You red or blue?' I asked. Well I didn't want to get off to a bad start by asking if he was a Blade or pig. His reply was 'Blade of course' Well that was it, within no time we were in the pub sharing stories. Top bloke and top place.
Apart from the football clubs that are a Global brand it means something when

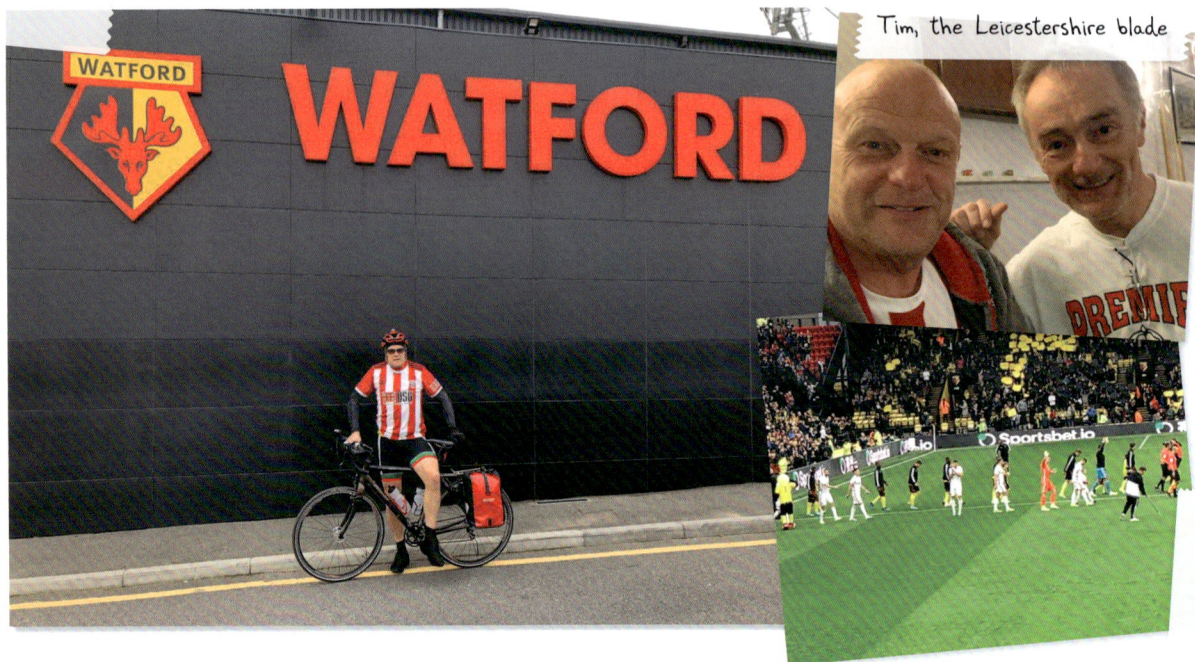

Tim, the Leicestershire blade

you're out of town or even Country and you see fellow fans. I hope we never get to the point where seeing Blades shirts like Man U becomes the norm. After another good chat with Tim over breakfast (hopefully going to his wedding in Thailand) it was back on the road. Slight drizzle but otherwise favourable conditions. Really enjoyed the route. You know, everyone should perhaps travel round our great country avoiding Motorways. Stopped half way at a magic cafe 'Dragonfly' having best tea cakes ever. 20 miles out I came across Kempston, naturally a quality Town.

I was on a particularly busy road at some lights when I noticed a mini bus full of school children. As my mental age is probably on a par with theirs it was only natural to wave and pull faces. I then unzipped my coat unveiling my 'Mr Happy' cycle shirt. The kids loved it and were all laughing. The overwhelming joy I felt for seeing all the kids laughing at me gave me an incredible amount of warmth inside. The B&B was in Whipsnade, and very nice indeed. A roaring fire greeted me which was lovely but sent a chilling reminder of what's to come over the next 6 cold months. After learning from my mistakes made on the opening 2 matches (leaving myself a lot of miles to do on the day of the match) I only had 20 miles to Vicarage Road. It was a lovely route mostly aside

Anne-Marie Burn (Watford FC)

a canal. I was ridiculously early so stopped at two cafes on route. Arriving just after 12 I got my usual photo then asked around for somewhere to plonk the grod. Watford were fantastic. They ushered me into an office and said I could leave it there. A lovely lady (Anne-Marie) said she would be there after the match to let me back in. I then went to seek out 'The Blades' pub. Good to see some familiar faces in there. Had a couple with Kevin Gage and his son Oliver who works for the FA in Canada, great chap. The match itself was a bit of a letdown to be honest but another point away from home leaving us disappointed is a sign of how far we've come.

After the match I went to get my bike and was delighted that Watford had left a signed shirt for me. What a fantastic gesture. A short ride to the station meant I could catch an earlier train. I then heard my name shouted. It was Paul Shields, a Blade I used to travel with who I'd not seen for about 20 years. Now we have seen some shite but had many laughs. Things are gathering momentum and most 'away' Blades know me now and keep throwing money at me. The feeling you get when complete strangers start waving money at you because of what your doing is very humbling. Not even sure they were all Blades.

WATFORD 0 BLADES 0

Dean Henderson played well after his costly error against Liverpool

No surprises as Henderson is back to his best

First he raised both arms aloft. Then, after checking the danger actually had passed, pointed a finger towards one corner of the Vicarage Road Stand where his name was being sung with gusto.

It was the first of two moments when Dean Henderson ensured Sheffield United would take at least a point from their latest Premier League fixture and, following the most challenging week of his career, proved one to sections of the commentariat.

After a costly error against Liverpool seven days earlier, the goalkeeper entered United's meeting with Watford under intense scrutiny. Not only did Henderson know further slips or mistakes would be analysed to the 'nth degree, he also understood they would be

used as evidence that Chris Wilder's critique of his previous performance had, as one news presenter rather hysterically suggested, threatened his mental wellbeing. It was, even for this confident 22-year-old, a huge weight to bear.

Henderson's response, which underlined why many believe he is an England player in waiting, came in the shape of an excellent save to deny Danny Welbeck before scrambling Craig Dawson's later header off the line.

Wilder was not surprised.

He said: "Nobody would be, not just me or the coaching staf. The reception Dean got, we all know about that relationship. He's been outstanding.

"I thought he looked a really good goalkeeper out there."

TEAMS

Watford: Foster, Janmaat, Prödl (Dawson 57), Cleverley, Welbeck (Sarr 77), Cathcart, Doucouré, Gray (Deulofeu 59), Holebas, Kabasele, Pereyra. **Unused:** Gomes, Chalobah, Hughes, Femenia.

Blades: Henderson, Baldock, Stevens, Fleck, O'Connell, Basham, Lundstram, McBurnie (Mousset 62), Robinson (Sharp 71), Egan, Norwood. **Unused:** L. Freeman, Jagielka, Osborn, Moore, Bešić.

Referee: Andre Marriner

STATS

WATFORD		BLADES
39	POSS %	61
8	SHOTS	9
2	SHOTS ON TARGET	3
7	CORNERS	7
7	FOULS	6

THAT'S NOT WAT BLADES EXPECTED

JAMES SHIELD
The Star's Blades writer

Email: james.shield@jpimedia.co.uk
Twitter: @JamesShield1

Nearly six months ago, when Chris Wilder first began plotting a course towards Premier League survival, he did not expect it to be quite like this.

The Sheffield United manager suspected opponents would try and bludgeon his newly promoted team into submission. Not, as Watford did on Saturday, flood their defence, sit back and lure them into a false sense of security before attempting to land a sucker punch.

Although the tactics Quique Sanchez Flores employed did not exactly make for an enthralling game, they did prove successful. The Spaniard's side overcame a difficult start before growing in stature as the match wore on and recording a first clean sheet in the league since February.

But Flores' strategy, partly designed to help his players recover from a woeful sequence of results, also represented a nod of respect towards the visitors. And, quite possibly, revealed how many opponents will look to handle a squad intent on attacking their way to safety.

After scaring but ultimately succumbing to Liverpool, the reigning European champions, Wilder appeared

as interested in the psychological challenge his men faced as he did the result. Which, like the hosts' under-conservative approach, was a measure of the speed with which they have adapted to life at the highest level.

"It was a little bit of a different pressure on us in a way, because people felt there was a result in there for us," Wildersaid. "Yes, because people look at league tables and current form. I don't know what the odds were but I'd have thought they were pretty tight for the home team and the away team. So we had to deal with that and the situation, where we were in control of the game but be aware of their major threats. Be aware of their great quality at the top of the pitch."

Watford, as Wilder alluded, are a club devoid of confidence rather than exceptional talent. Nine of those who began the meeting with United were internationals, including former Arsenal striker Danny Welbeck. Ismaila Sarr, a £30m signing from Rennes, was introduced as a substitute. Given Flores' employers still prop up the rest of the table.

There were flashes of their quality during a largely forgettable contest, but Watford focused on stifling

Oli McBurnie received precious little reward for his efforts

United's creativity. There were times when it seemed as if their three centre-halves and two full-backs had been instructed not to stray beyond the penalty area.

"I was pleased with the performance but disappointed with the result, and that shows how far we've come," Wilder said. "Against a team that was playing on the counter attack and desperate for its first win of the season."

Had United shown a little bit more care with their final balls, they might well have taken three points.

Oli McBurnie and Callum Robinson worked tirelessly, but were effectively suffocated.

It would also be remiss not to concede that Watford also had the better chances, with Dean Henderson thwarting Welbeck and Craig Cathcart after Andre Gray missed a sitter.

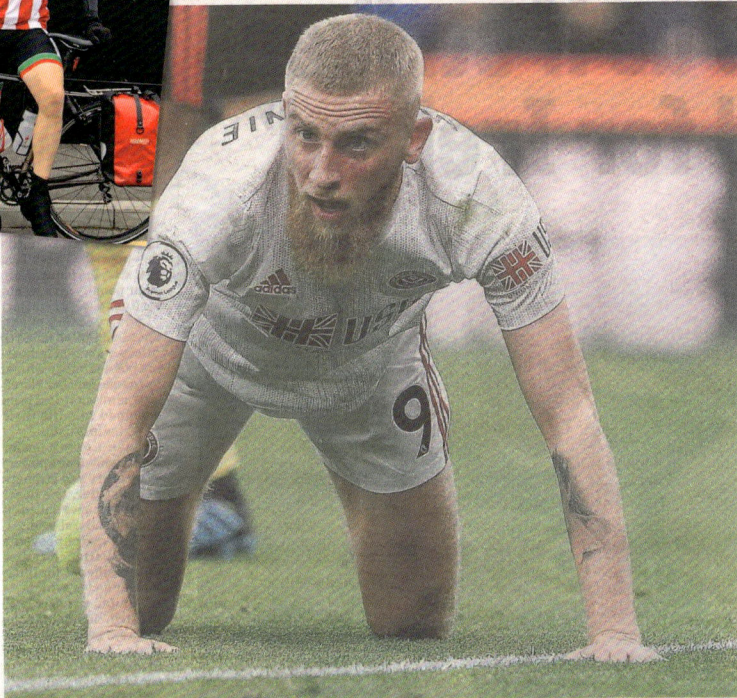

Frustration shows for Blades striker Oli McBurnie

Callum Robinson had no reward for his efforts

John Fleck worked hard to drive United on

PLAYER RATINGS

HENDERSON — 8
What a way to bounce back from last week's error. Made a superb stop to deny Welbeck and then denied Dawson.

BALDOCK — 7
Looked frustrated with his teammates as moves broke down and got up and down the pitch as well as ever.

BASHAM — 7
Had an early dodgy moment against Andre Gray but put in a good cross which McBurnie was inches away from.

EGAN — 7
Headed everything that came his way and dealt well with the threats of Welbeck and Gray amongst others.

O'CONNELL — 7
Survived an injury scare in the second half when he stayed down, holding his ribs before coming on after treatment.

STEVENS — 7
Didn't give Janmaat a moment's peace down the left and came inside to hammer one shot over Foster's goal.

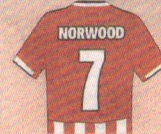

NORWOOD — 7
Recycled the ball intelligently to keep United in possession but almost let in Watford with an underhit pass to Lundstram.

LUNDSTRAM — 7
An energetic display from the midfielder from the right channel, getting on the ball as often as he could.

FLECK — 8
Drove United on and one mazy run in the first half saw him beat two or three players before finally being stopped.

MCBURNIE — 6
A frustrating afternoon for the striker, summed up when he was booked for a late challenge on Doucoure.

ROBINSON — 6
Caught a volley well from McBurnie's knockdown but fired it straight at Foster, who gathered after flicking it into his face.

SUBSTITUTES

LYS MOUSSET 6
A couple of delightful turns and flicks got him away from his marker a couple of times

BILLY SHARP 6
Made his first appearance back after his ban to a great ovation from the away end

HIGHLIGHT
Watford's decision to play on the counter-attack at Vicarage Road, rather than adopt a more pro-active approach, was a nod to the progress Sheffield United have made since returning to the Premier League. The hosts might be low on confidence, but they still possess some excellent individual talents. After studying United's performance against Liverpool a week earlier, where they came within a whisker of becoming the first team this season to take points off the European champions, Quique Sanchez Flores decided it would be too dangerous for his team to try and take the game to the visitors. United should take it as a compliment.

LOWLIGHT
United worked themselves into some excellent positions. But too often their final ball was poor. First, that let opponents who despite flooding their defence looked scared to death at the back, off the the hook. Then, as the afternoon wore on, it provided them with the encouragement to commit more men forward themselves. It also meant Callum Robinson and Oli McBurnie in particular, despite some tireless running, were seldom able to escape their markers' clutches. And yes, that was 'markers' plural. Even though United dominated both territory and possession at Vicarage Road, Flores' side actually enjoyed the better chances.

CHAPTER 5

West Ham United, 26th October

Jeez, just sat (Wednesday) looking at the forecast and feeling like Man Flu is taking hold.

Thankfully I set off (Thursday) and although overcast and cool no rain as yet. The air seemed heavy. I noticed more than ever the fumes from cars exhausts. Maybe cos it was rush hour. The man flu, fingers crossed, has not took hold yet but when I set off I sounded like one of my Dads old Cortinas, coughing and spluttering. I pulled the choke out and all was good. It didn't take long for the rain to start. It got heavier and lasted all day. This was the first ride that I really had to dig deep and go into my cycling trance. I thought about the poorly children and what their parents must be going through. All of a sudden I wasn't wet and cold anymore. I always find it helps to set little targets when on a longer ride. With 35 miles to go I made a deal with my legs that I would find a cafe when I got to under 25 to go. It was actually 20 to go when I found a nice cafe in a garden centre. As I got served I said to the guy behind

Lola wants to come with daddy!

the counter 'this is the best cafe in the world' that was before I ate anything. Just get me out of the rain. Eventually arrived at Corby at the B&B. The bath was simply the best. As I was literally in the middle of nowhere I ordered a Chinese takeaway. Had a good nights sleep and woke to no rain yeah: shame I couldn't stay longer as another great host. Set off and felt strong. Meeting Cousin Sam at Kimbolton (24 miles) so got a lick on. Always nice to ride with someone. Arrived in good time although noticed the headwind was getting stronger. Nice place Kimbolton, you could smell money in the air. Sam cycled with me to St Neots where

we stopped for brunch with Auntie Anne, Uncle Bernard and Hannah. Don't usually stop so early in a ride (half way) but lovely to see them. I got going and the rain held off for at least 2 miles! Then omg it was like cycling in a shower with a jumbo jets engines blowing in my face. I'd allowed another stop with 15 to go but there was no shop or cafe. I was that wet I swear I could taste Chlorine. All of a sudden I was struggling, and I mean struggling. O shit I'm in trouble.

I needed fuel. I started shouting at myself to stay alert and even started

singing old Blades songs. 'Ken McNaught Ken McNaught he's the best player United's ever bought, he scores with his head, he scores with his foot, he's so good he can score with his.........'
At last a shop. Fuelled up and crept to the hotel. Checked in and was told to drive to the Garden Court, 'drive' I said. It was another half a mile away ffs. Maybe an age thing but these large corporate hotels are not my thing anymore. Give me a nice friendly B&B every day. As I walked the mile to breakfast I looked up at the sky, mmm them bloody clouds are moving quick. Will set off at 10 so can watch first half of egg chasing semi final. England v New Zealand.

Set off and couldn't bloody find the way out of the grounds. Eventually got on the trail only to be obstructed by a tree which had been blown over. The wind was blowing so strong, against as normal. Really tired. Am I too old or are the past two days catching up with me? Seemed to take a while but eventually arrived. Met up with a few West Ham fans who were great characters. Saw Harry Basset and TC.
Met up with Mike from the Dronfield Eye. A few Blades stopped to get pictures with me. One a lovely girl called Sarah who is also friends with Paul (my mate). At least the story is out there, now to push the donations. Found a place to plonk the bike but

the organisation was appalling. People working at a football ground who haven't a clue about football fans. Made it in and met up with Wayne, Angie and few others. The ground is and will always be an athletic stadium. I feel so sorry for the West Ham fans. They've had their souls ripped out. The Blades fans taunted 'You're not West Ham anymore.' Harsh but so very true. Chris Wilder needed a taxi from the dug out to the side of the pitch. I asked a steward where I could buy a programme and he just replied 'sorry I don't know what that is' The first half was very defensive by the Blades and we were holding out well until Snodgrass found space and eased it passed Deano. A player I've always admired, probably cos he always performs well against us. The second half saw us completely go for it. Billy came on then the Moose and in no time I was being embraced by a guy who looked and smelt like he'd been drinking for a week. We held out and infact, could have grabbed a winner. Still undefeated away. This cycling lark is bringing them luck. Jordan had managed to get hold of a ticket with his brother Ryan, so the plan was to come back with them. I

didn't account for them not knowing where they had left the car. Hilarious, trying not to show my utter disbelief. I kept asking, ' but surely you know what car park you're in?'. After walking about an hour they found it. Really ffs. All night I haven't stopped thinking about what the West Ham owners have done to their club. So very sad, especially as Upton Park was the complete opposite. If the Blades hierarchy ever move us from BDTBL that's me done. After just witnessing the Blades destruction of Burnley I can now make a very bold statement, 'This is the best time I've known being a Blade.' My first match was against Man City in the Texaco Cup in 1974. I stood on a box behind my Dad on the old John Street Terrace. We won 4-2. What a journey since!

WEST HAM 1 BLADES 1

Lys Mousset celebrates scoring the equalising goal at West Ham

Mousset earns deserved draw for Wilder's men

Styles make fights and, if Manuel Pellegrini's pre-match analysis was to be believed, this fixture should have been a battle between eleven purists and opponents who favour what Nigel Benn might describe as a good old fashioned tear-up.

Instead the West Ham manager, who had described Sheffield United beforehand as a "typically English team", watched a finish oozing lashings of technical brilliance secure the visitors a draw at the London Stadium.

Trailing to a Robert Snodgrass goal and with their superb away record hanging precariously in the balance, Lys Mousset ensured Swansea City remain the last club to have beaten United on the road when, nine months after

that defeat at the Liberty Stadium, he stepped-off the bench and caressed the ball beyond Roberto Jiménez Gago to stun the home crowd.

It proved a deserved reward for performance laden with character and, given the bizarre scouting reports his analysts had concocted, a thoroughly confusing conclusion for Pellegrini.

"I thought he took it brilliantly," Enda Stevens said, after providing the assist for Mousset's strike following Issa Diop's indecisive clearance. "I never expected him to shoot but, the second it left his boot, you could tell it was going in the bottom corner. He made the most of it superbly."

TEAMS

West Ham: Jiménez, Zabaleta, Balbuena, Diop, Cresswell, Rice, Yarmolenko, Noble (Fornals 78), Snodgrass (Ajeti 86), Felipe Anderson (Lanzini 66), Haller. Substitutes: C Sánchez, Ogbonna, Fredericks, Martin.

Sheff Utd: Henderson, Basham, Egan, O'Connel, Baldock, Lundstram, Norwood (Mousset 63), Fleck, Stevens, McGoldrick (Besic 81), Robinson (Sharp 54). Substitutes: Freeman, McBurnie, Moore.

Referee: David Coote (Notts)

Attendance: 59,878

STATS

HAMMERS		BLADES
61	POSS %	39
12	SHOTS	10
4	SHOTS ON TARGET	4
10	CORNERS	4
7	FOULS	10

LYS SIMP DEMANDS ATTENTION

JAMES SHIELD
The Star's Blades writer
Email: james.shield@jpimedia.co.uk
Twitter: @JamesShield1

The London Stadium does not lend itself to football.

What happens on the pitch, separated from the stands by an expanse of claret carpet, can make the actual match action feel incidental.

But in Lys Mousset, Sheffield United have acquired a player who simply demands attention. Be it by driving his Lamborghini sports car or, as happened on Saturday afternoon, producing superb finishes which decide the outcome of Premier League games.

The Frenchman's strike at West Ham, who appeared to be edging towards victory thanks to Robert Snodgrass' first-half effort, was reward for a combative if not entirely convincing performance from the visitors. It also, following his match-winning effort against Arsenal five days earlier, confirmed Mousset does not simply possess pace and raw, unadulterated power. He is equipped with a high level of technical expertise too.

"Lys came on and he gives us that explosiveness up top," his colleague Enda Stevens said. And I thought he took his goal really well.

"He is going to be a real threat for us this season, they all are. We have got great

strikers. Each and every single one of them play their part."

As Stevens pointed-out, United have accumulated a variety of different attacking options since being promoted last season. Billy Sharp is a poacher, David McGoldrick a creator while new arrivals Callum Robinson and Oli McBurnie provide industry and work rate. But for the time being at least, it is Mousset who is dominating the headlines having initially, following his sumer move from AFC Bournemouth, been something of a slow-burner.

The fact Chris Wilder chose to start him on the bench, after his exploits earlier in the week, confirmed fitness remains an issue.

"He is just a normal, laid-back guy," Stevens continued. "He has bought in to what we are about and he is working hard on it.

"And you can see that by his performances. He is on form now and he will only get better for us I think. He has got great English. He gets involved with the lads and loves being around us and I think he is really enjoying himself."

Despite appearing to acclimatise to life in the top-flight with encouraging ease – they

ended the contest ranked seventh in the table – United remain a squad greater than the sum of its parts.

So perhaps it was fitting, even though Mousset landed the most telling blow on a West Ham side with designs of qualifying for Europe, that one of his team mates emerged as the driving force behind this result.

Previously an unheralded figure at Bramall Lane, John Lundstram has instead become central to Wilder's plans. His contribution in the capital, assisting his defenders as the hosts controlled the first-half before surging forward with venom as United seized the momentum after the break, was absolutely vital.

Best known for his energy, Lundstram also delivered some excellent crosses into the box, although it was Stevens who provided the assist for Mousset.

Lys Mousset all smiles after his leveller

Me with Jordan (hey dude, wher's my car?)

George Baldock of Sheffield United fires in a cross against West Ham

Sheffield United's David McGoldrick at the London Stadium

Jack O'Connell of Sheffield United heads the ball at goal

PLAYER RATINGS

HENDERSON 7
Left badly exposed for West Ham's opener but made a good save from Anderson after United were caught on break.

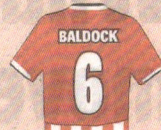

BALDOCK 6
Had a good chance to equalise but was denied by goalkeeper Roberto. Skewed another good opening wide later on.

BASHAM 6
Wasn't too convincing with his header in the move that led to West Ham's opener but almost set up a goal with superb cross.

EGAN 6
Couldn't get across to stop Snodgrass putting the Hammers ahead but was otherwise his normal commanding self.

O'CONNELL 6
Showed good defensive instincts to not dive in against lively Yarmolenko and did well to contain West Ham's threats.

STEVENS 6
Intelligent use of his body and a deft header for Mousset's equaliser and the most professional of fouls to bring down Haller.

LUNDSTRAM 7
Couple of superb individual bits of play, including a beautiful backheel to allow Fleck to cross for Baldock.

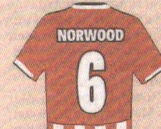

NORWOOD 6
Caught in possession by Anderson which led to a good chance for the Brazilian, before Henderson saved well.

FLECK 7
Quiet in the first half, very good in the second. His delivery was good from set-plays, almost setting up McGoldrick.

ROBINSON 6
Missed golden chance from Basham's cross, although slight touch from goalkeeper Roberto may have played a part.

MCGOLDRICK 6
Had the best chance of the first half when a corner fell to him, but his flick was saved by Roberto.

SUBSTITUTES

BILLY SHARP 6
Gave United a spark when he came off the bench

LYS MOUSSET 7
Made an impact once again with a bobbling volley that went in.

MO BESIC N/A
Helped see out the game.

CHAPTER 6

Tottenham Hotspur, 9th November

The forecast all week was changing constantly, I'm sure Michael Fish (other than Hurricane gate) was more accurate than today's forecasters, even with all the modern day Technology. In summary, I'm gonna get wet!

I dropped Lola off earlier as I'd lost an hours daylight in the afternoon. I had that many layers on I looked a ringer for Mitchelin man. Good I did as the rain was constant and heavy. After about 25 miles I came to a familiar sight, the road flooded! Only up to my shin this time so happy days. I was cycling up hill, against the wind and against a torrent of water running down the hills. I stopped for a coffee at a shop at 30 miles as my hands were that cold I couldn't change my gears into the top chain ring. I thought back to last summer when one day in Portugal I cycled in 45 degree heat. Thinking about it didn't warm me up I'm afraid. Setting little targets, I decided lunch would be at

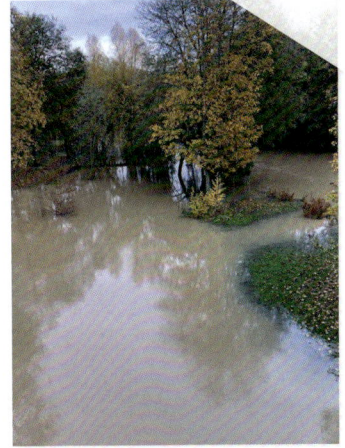

50 miles. The rain was actually easing off, or maybe that was wishful thinking. Stopped at a nice pub and I peeled off some layers and attempted to dry them. With 25 miles left (a distance that normally would be rattled off in no time) I needed motivation so, as I was on Country lanes I put some music on, stuck my Beats in and pressed play. Thought I'd go back to my youth with some Status Quo, that would get me moving. FFS, first song that came on, 'Rain', you could not make it up! It took me a while to peel my clothes off. My bedroom for the night looked more like a laundrette. Well 'The Quo' certainly pushed me hard, the lactic acid in my legs kept me awake for long periods of the night, damn you Francis Rossi! Looking at today's forecast (Friday) most of the country is going to be

dry except for, it seems, the 70 mile strip I will be on. Really? The rain actually didn't arrive today (Friday) thank goodness. In fact the big yellow ball in the sky nearly made a showing. I stopped at a lovely cafe, The Courtyard in Papworth. From the moment I walked in I sensed the warmth this place gave. People all looked happy and laughing. I had a chat with the owner (an Ipswich fan) and within a couple of minutes he was putting £10 in my hand. Fabulous gesture. My pace was very quick so I decided to stop again for a cuppa at the Sunflower tea room, Hare Street. All of a sudden I felt terrible, dizzy. For the remaining miles I was really worried I was going to flake out. Arriving at the Hotel checking in I was in serious trouble. Managed to make it to my room. Really

need to get right for the morning.
Ok, so it seems I have a bug/virus.
Amazing that if I was at home and
was going to go to the gym how
there's no way I could make it.
Not sure what was in the air this
morning but I felt like Bruce Willis in
Sixth Sense. Everyone I said something
to just looked through me. Shit this bug
must have killed me and I'm a ghost!
Cycling through Lee Valley was lovely
if not freezing. Boating life always
seems so chilled out. I now know why
as all I could smell was weed!
A steady 20 miles saw me arrive at the
amazing White Hart Lane, sorry but that's
what it is to me. Without doubt the best
new ground I've been to. However, and I
really hoped there wouldn't be a 'however',
some of the protocols were beyond belief.
I was about to enter the ground and
was told I couldn't take my pannier in

the ground and I would have to go to
'bag drop'. Bag drop, bleeding hell, what's
happening. After 45 minutes waiting
I eventually was relieved of £10 and
provided with a swimmers band, marvellous.
Once in the ground I was very
impressed with the set up. Even the
beer filled the glass from the bottom.
A far cry from BDTBL, although
I know where I'd rather be.
The Blades are on fire, better team
by a long way. Then mid way through
the second half Spurs seemed to
pounce and went 1-0 up. Not deserved.
This group of players and management
don't give up so I wasn't too downbeat.
Then a swift move down the right
saw a cross put in and Didzy poked
it in. We all went barmy, including a
few Blades in corporate behind us.
The players were all stood waiting for
the restart and then the 'checking

VAR' came on the big screen. After what seemed and agonising wait, unbelievably the goal was ruled out because Lundstrams Movember was offside. I really think this one incident will force the powers that be to rethink the whole thing.

This got the lads going even more and it wasn't long till Baldy crossed and the ball ended up in the net. Yes I went barmy but slightly subdued as they were checking VAR again. This time we could go barmy twice. What a performance, it gets better every week. Dreamland!

I ran out on the full time whistle as I had to collect my bag. Great to hear the Spurs fans saying we are top 6 material. Then the 7 mile cycle through a rainy North London to St Pancras. Get there in good time, to find lots of people waiting around. Walk up to the information board to find the 18.31 has been cancelled. O for Christ's sake. A fellow Blade came up and suggested we take the next Derby train and take it from there. Fortunately there was a train going to Chesterfield so all's well that ends well. A visit to Chester's fish bar on route home did the trick. Legs very heavy, body very tired but it was all worth it. One thing I've learnt over the past few years is that when you're low dig very deep and physically punish yourself, I guarantee your mental tiredness will be replaced by a soothing aching body. Never in my most far fetched dreams have we drawn to Man Utd, dominated for 80 minutes and been thoroughly disappointed at only gaining a point. As we approach December 2019 we sit 6th in the Premier League. 3 years ago we had just managed to get in to the top 6 of Division 3. Can we dare to dream that this journey will continue?

SPURS 1 BLADES 1

DECISION NO GOAL — VAR — 63:14

The Blades' 'equaliser' is ruled out by VAR

'Different-sized boot' makes all the difference

Speaking before a match influenced by one of their player's shoe size as well as moments of brilliance and a rare defensive lapse, Mauricio Pochettino had compared Sheffield United to a rugby team because of their fighting spirit.

It was a well-meaning comment, designed to highlight their character and togetherness, but given the hackneyed narrative which followed his squad's rise out of the Championship, it appeared to reopen old wounds for Chris Wilder when relayed to him afterwards.

This he reminded, head bowed and sighing outside Tottenham's media suite, had been trying to convey

George Baldock, however, knew different. Revealing details of

TEAMS

Tottenham Hotspur: Gaazaniga, Sanchez, Son, Kane, Dier, Sissoko, Lo Celso, Alli (Foth 72), Aurier (Moura 86), Ndombele (Winks 46), Davies. Not used: Vorm, Alderweireld, Sessegnon, Eriksen.

Sheffield United: Henderson, Basham, Egan, O;Connell, Stevens, Baldock, Norwood, Fleck, Lundstram, McGoldrick (LFreeman 90), Mousset (Robinson 88). Not used: Moore, McBurnie, Sharp, Jagielka, Besic.

Referee: Graham Scott (Oxfordshire).

a post-game chat with a former MK Dons teammate Dele Alli, the United wing-back explained the Argentine and his players had been trying to convey respect.

Baldock said: "He's watched us a few times on the television and he's been surprised with how well we've played. It's lovely to hear things like that from such a top-quality player."

Baldock gave his view on VAR after David McGoldrick's disallowed goal.

"It has its pros and cons and Saturday was bitterly disappointing. The margin, it's just a different sized boot, isn't it? I suppose the talk will be about VAR but I went home revelling in getting a point here, not the fact that VAR's killed us."

STATS

SPURS		BLADES
61	POSS %	39
17	SHOTS	14
5	SHOTS ON TARGET	4
4	CORNERS	4
6	FOULS	9

COURAGEOUS BLADES EARN THEIR SPURS

JAMES SHIELD
The Star's Blades writer
Email: james.shield@jpimedia.co.uk
Twitter: @JamesShield1

More than their victory over Arsenal or performance against European Champions Liverpool, this was the moment which revealed why Sheffield United have adapted so quickly to Premier League football.

Courage, determination, focus and a true sense of purpose condensed into one 20-minute period.

After falling behind at Tottenham Hotspur and then seeing David McGoldrick's 'equaliser' wiped from the scoresheet by VAR, Chris Wilder's players could easily have crumbled under a weight of disappointment inside the hosts' cavernous arena.

Instead, displaying great psychological fortitude and no little skill, they kept on pressing, kept on believing before eventually finding a way back into the contest when George Baldock restored parity following Heung-Min Son's opener.

His finish not only lifted United to fifth in the table, just seven months after being promoted, it also ensured an unbeaten away record stretching back to January remained intact.

"It was one of the things

that I admitted during the build-up, at times it's not always a win you feel more satisfied with," Wilder said. "This is certainly up there with the outstanding performances we've had on the road during my time at the football club. From Enda's mistake – he's not made many by the way – then to score a great goal, to see it chalked off, and then go again."

The error Wilder was referring to came early in the second-half when Stevens, who as his manager underlined has made precious few in United colours, tried to pass the ball to John Egan rather than simply clear his lines. It was a misjudgement, but not nearly as big a one as some of those made by the match officials. The visitors were left bewildered by Jonathan Moss's interpretation of events during the build-up to McGoldrick's strike.

Taking nearly four minutes to disallow the centre-forward's effort from his video analysis suite at Stockley Park, the 49-year-old's decision to rule John Lundstram had strayed offside during the build-up not only appeared harsh, but also seemed to contravene competition guidelines about how the review system should be employed.

Wilder was understandably still frustrated when he discussed it afterwards.

He said: "It does frustrate the players because we should be talking about them, about the upcoming game and how well they've done. It will nick a bit of the limelight but hopefully it won't because I thought they were outstanding. To come here, and perform like that, it wasn't a backs-to-the-wall performance by any means."

Wilder was delighted with his players' response to going behind.

He said: "We didn't just boot it clear and chase after it. There was a lot of talk about us at the start of the season. But I'm delighted with the attitude of the players, how they crack on and push again. There was no panic in our play when we went 1-0 down. Instead, I thought we always looked as if we could get back into the game."

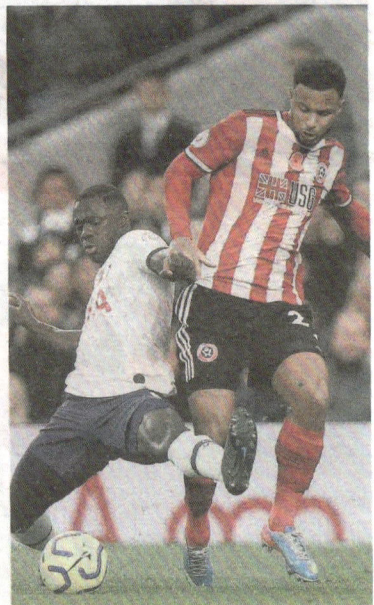
Blades striker Lys Mousset is challenged by Davinson Sanchez

Sheffield United's George Baldock (second left) celebrates scoring his side's equaliser at the Tottenham Hotspur Stadium

David McGoldrick celebrates the 'goal' that was eventually ruled out by VAR after nearly four minutes

PLAYER RATINGS

HENDERSON 7

Couldn't do anything about Son's goal, which also took a slight deflection off Basham

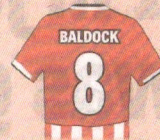

BALDOCK 8

Signalled his intentions in the first minute with a driving run. Scored equaliser with a cross-come-shot to earn point

BASHAM 7

Given a difficult time early on by Dele Alli but hardly put a foot wrong after that. A superb challenge to deny Son late on

EGAN 7

Played a part in Spurs' opener as he suffered a mix-up with his Irish mate Stevens. Kept Harry Kane quiet

O'CONNELL 7

Was robbed in possession by Kane on the halfway line late in the game – the only time Kane got the better of him

STEVENS 7

Partly culpable for Spurs' opener but almost redeemed himself with a superb cross for McGoldrick's 'goal'

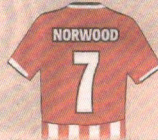

NORWOOD 7

Saw an early effort touched over the bar by Gazzaniga and kept United ticking over in midfield

FLECK 7

Looked disappointed with himself as an early effort on his left foot was saved by Gazzaniga. Linked up well down the left

LUNDSTRAM 7

So close to another goal in the first half when he glanced Stevens' cross wide, and then thumped the outside of post

MCGOLDRICK 8

Thought he had got United back on level terms when he netted at the back post, before VAR ruled it out

MOUSSET 8

Showed pace and power in another impressive showing. Almost scored when he turned Sanchez, but shot wide

SUBSTITUTES

CALLUM ROBINSON

Came on for Mousset late on as United looked to see out the game

LUKE FREEMAN

Replaced David McGoldrick who earned a deserved standing ovation

HIGHLIGHT

Sheffield United were caught by a number of blows during this fixture, although not all of them were landed by Tottenham Hotspur.

The one which led to Heung-Min Son's goal was self-inflicted – with Enda Stevens trying to pass to a team mate rather than clear his lines – while VAR official Jonthan Moss caught them with another when he disallowed, after a near four-minute break, David McGoldrick's 'equaliser'.

Although the effort from George Baldock which eventually ensured United took a point from the game might have been a touch fortuitous, that slice of luck was deserved.

LOWLIGHT

Neither VAR official Jonathan Moss nor referee Graham Scott covered themselves in glory on Saturday afternoon.

Moss'decision to rule John Lundstram had strayed offside before McGoldrick turned home Stevens' cross seemed plain wrong at worst and mistaken at best.

It seems strange that, after being told only clear and obvious errors would be over turned, it took over three minutes for a decision to be reached.

Scott raised eyebrows when, having already booked Eric Dier, he refused to show a second yellow card for bringing down Lys Mousset.

Wolverhampton Wanderers, 1st December

A long time Blade friend Paul has lived in Wolverhampton for many a year so I planned to stay at his on the Saturday. 70 miles, was in the day doable, or was it?

Waking up early Saturday morning (the game had been put back to Sunday as Wolves played on the Thursday in the Europa League), and looking outside my heart sank. Everywhere was white over. The hardest frost of the Autumn so far. I planned to set off at 8.30 but waited a little longer to allow the sun to come up. Setting off down my road it wasn't long before I felt the wheels sliding. I got off and walked down the rest of the hill. I took it very steady as I rode through Chesterfield. The fog then started descending as I climbed into the Peaks. As I levelled out there was a sharp left bend, I approached slowly but not slow enough. My front wheel went and within a second I was in the hedgerow. My first

tumble, nothing damaged on bike and no injuries to me. I've always hated the slightest noise from my bike so shortly after my tumble I was really wound up when there was an awful grinding noise from my back wheel. Then when I looked, to my horror the rear brake blocks had frozen to the wheel. No wonder my legs were struggling. It took me nearly 3 hours to get to Darley Dale, partly because I had to walk a mile down hill. I met a good friend, Trudi, in Darley Dale. We decided to go a little further and stopped at a pub, The Hollybush near Winster. The owners were quality and provided free coffee and biscuits, great gesture. A Mansfield Town fan. I said my goodbyes to Trudi and set off.

The sun had at last broken through the fog and it was very pleasant indeed. Paul had planned to cycle to meet me 20 miles from the finish. I started pushing it a little harder making the most of the much improved conditions. Ahead I noticed a wall of cloud again and within no time the sun was gone and it was like stepping into a freezer. It was probably the coldest I've ever been on a bike. I got to Cannock Chase, which looked gorgeous even in the pea souper I was now in. Eventually met Paul with 15 to go. The previous 20 was tough and the mileage was slow to be ticked off. Once riding with Paul we seemed to be finished in no time. First ride where I finished in the dark.

Great night with Paul reminiscing about all the away games we've been to and how bad we were. It was brilliant to wake knowing I only had a couple of miles to ride to the ground. The sky was blue and sun was out and Blades are in town, happy days. I stepped outside Paul's house and unbelievably it started drizzling, ffs, Paul joked I was like the character on Charlie Brown with a rain cloud constantly over him. It soon stopped and I was soon outside the Billy Wright Stand. I feel a close bond with Wolves, similar recent years. What really annoys me is how just because Arsenal are searching for a new manager the TV guys just go on tipping Nuno Santos because Arsenal are top 6. Well it's time there was a new top 6 such as Leicester, Wolves and who knows one day us. Met Jordan and Ryan outside the ground then walked to where they'd left the car, yes they remembered where it was this time. Had a couple of beers and saw a few guys I knew. The Police were top notch, very engaging and respectful. After walking back to the ground and just about to enter Jordan realises he had left his ticket in the car....yes guys that's my future

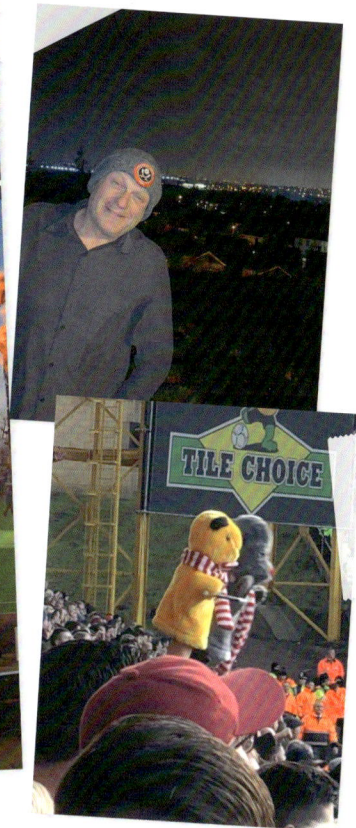

son in law. Top lad really.

Can't really say 'took my seat' cos we don't sit at away matches. Even if we did we would soon be up as the Moose was at it again, first couple of minutes and we're 1-0 up. Cracking. Lord knows why they checked with VAR but we're getting used to this, feels like a wind up now. Superb start, I definitely would take a point so to go in at half time 1 up was a huge bonus. Not sure whether it was the fact it was Sunday afternoon or the away end spreads the length of the pitch but we seemed quieter than normal. Wolves equalised giving

me a sinking feeling. However the boys fought hard and could have won if we had taken the chances. A thoroughly brilliant, brave performance. Home in quick time and reunited with my Lola. First time I've got less than a week till my next journey. Please don't judge but just watching I'm a Celebrity and Ian Wright just left. Initially I wasn't his biggest fan but he's just said something that has won me over. 'I've learnt a lot about myself and still have work to do' top man. I completely relate to that as I'm really finding a lot out about myself and also have work to do, 100% me.

WOLVES 1 BLADES 1

Blades boss Chris Wilder during the Molineux clash

'Greedy' Wilder disappointed to miss out on win

A fifth goal in as many Premier League starts for Lys Mousset helped Sheffield United secure a creditable point at Wolverhampton Wanderers.

Chris Wilder's side had chances to extend their lead after the centre-forward's early finish, with David McGoldrick drawing a smart save before Matt Doherty equalised for Wolverhampton Wanderers.

So although the final scoreline will have been tinged with frustration, Wilder acknowledged the progress his squad has made since being promoted last term.

"I don't want to be greedy," he said. "But we were disappointed not to take all three points, even against a very good side who I have a lot of respect for. It's a good result for us. But we always want to drive it forward and, even though they could have maybe nicked it at the end, we felt we could have been in a slightly stronger position by then."

Early in the second half David McGoldrick found himself in space but could not beat the Wolves goalkeeper, before Mousset also sliced high and wide.

Wolves took advantage of those reprieves when Doherty turned home Jiminez's 64th minute cross. "They (United) are very good," said Wolves manager Nuno Espirito Santo. "So I was pleased we stayed in it and competed until the very end."

TEAMS

Wolverhampton Wanderers: Patricio, Doherty, Neves, Jiminez, Coady, Jota, Jonny, Moutinho, Dendoncker, Traore, Kilman. Not used: Ruddy, Vallejn, Neto, Cutrone, Vinagre, Otasowie, Cundle.

Sheffield United: Henderson, Basham, Egan, O'Connell, Stevens, Baldock, Norwood, Fleck, Lundstram (L Freeman 90), McGoldrick (McBurnie 72), Mousset (Robinson 86). Not used: Moore, L Freeman, Sharp, Robinson, Jagielka, Besic.

Referee: David Coote (Nottinghamshire).

Attendance: 31,642

STATS

WOLVES		BLADES
60	POSS %	40
13	SHOTS	9
3	SHOTS ON TARGET	4
7	CORNERS	2
12	FOULS	18

RESPECT FOR INCREDIBLE PROGRESS

JAMES SHIELD
The Star's Blades writer

Email: james.shield@jpimedia.co.uk
Twitter: @JamesShield1

Two seasons ago, Chris Wilder stood in awe on the touchline as Diogo Jota sliced open Sheffield United's defence and scored Wolverhampton Wanderers' second goal of what would prove a 3-0 victory.

The finish was good. The build up even better as the hosts, who would go on to lift the Championship title, proved they were too slick and too clever for second tier football.

Only 21 months and 80 games later, United prepared for this fixture sixth in the Premier League. Only a point and a place behind Nuno Espirito Santo's side, the speed of their progress, like the Portuguese's strike on that February evening, is best described as remarkable.

Although the action was compelling - ebbing and flowing as Lys Mousset and Matt Doherty traded goals - it was the contrasting methods these two clubs employ behind the scenes which, at least before kick-off, piqued peoples' interest.

Wolves, owned by a Chinese conglomerate and effectively controlled by one of the game's most powerful agents, have established themselves in the top-flight by flexing their financial muscles. United, whose budget is dwarfed by the majority of their rivals, rely on intelligence gathering; identifying players from the lower divisions with the potential to perform at the highest level.

"It's important you ultimately don't look at wage bills, budgets, the names on the back of shirts and the badges on the front," Wilder had said beforehand. "We don't and that has been our approach all the way through. When we first stepped into the Championship, as we all know, people weren't scared of telling us that we'd get eaten up. People were telling us from about two miles away. But here we are now, in this position. Still, I don't want to take a backwards step and the players don't either. Respect has to be earned and that usually comes at the end of games, not at the beginning of them."

United had certainly earnt Nuno's by the time referee David Cootes brought proceedings to a close, with the Portuguese describing them as a "very good team" prepared to fight until the bitter end. The same could be said of Wolves who kept plugging away after surviving a series of scares to take

John Fleck challenges Matt Doherty of Wolves in the air

something from a fixture staged less than 72 hours following their Europa League tie with Braga. On this occasion it was United's tactical discipline which impressed. Mousset's strike, his fifth in as many league starts for the club, provided them with a platform upon which to build. Doherty punished United's failure to stretch their advantage immediately after the break, with David McGoldrick and Mousset failing to find the back of the net after being presented with opportunities. But Wolves were also unable to properly exploit the possession they enjoyed thanks to United's defensive shape. It was further proof they are becoming more sophisticated by the week, no longer reliant upon being able to overwhelm opponents with their attacking wing-backs and over-lapping centre-halves.

Lys Mousset celebrates his second-minute goal with his delighted teammates

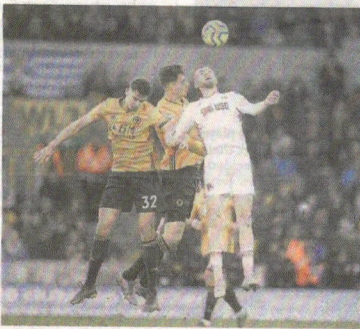

Oli McBurnie and Leander Dendoncker of Wolves

Dean Henderson saves smartly at his near post

PLAYER RATINGS

HENDERSON 7
Good early save from Jiminez's header. Handling and kicking generally good and could do little to nothing about the goal

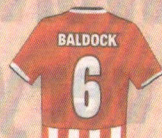

BALDOCK 6
Got forward at will in the first half. Perhaps fortunate not to see red when he brought down Jota again later in the game

BASHAM 8
Showed great defensive instincts early on to get across and snuff out the danger. Then did so two or three times more.

EGAN 8
Returned to the United side and looked like he'd never been away. One challenge to deny Jimenez was a real beauty.

O'CONNELL 7
The usual consistent performance from O'Connell, until a second-half booking blotted his copybook a little.

STEVENS 6
Beaten by international colleague Doherty early on down the right. Aside from a few flashes, didn't hit usual heights.

LUNDSTRAM 7
Showed several neat touches, as well as a bit of bite when United didn't have it. Sheer desire to chase summed him up.

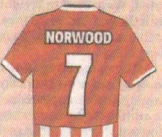

NORWOOD 7
The captain was good with and without the ball, putting his body on the line when needed to stop Wolves' attacks.

FLECK 7
Saw a good chance to make it 2-0 in the first half saved by Patricio after a good pass from Mousset.

MCGOLDRICK 7
Enjoyed at least two good chances to get on the scoresheet but is still waiting for first top flight goal.

MOUSSET 7
Put United ahead early and almost added a second instantly. But overhit a couple of passes when United were well placed.

SUBSTITUTES
OLI MCBURNIE N/A
Almost scored a winner late on, heading over the bar

CALLUM ROBINSON N/A
Came on too late to have any real influence in the game

LUKE FREEMAN N/A
Came on too late to have any real influence in the game

HIGHLIGHT
Lots have already pretended that, even though he barely started a game for AFC Bournemouth, they were aware of his talents and potential. But in truth, few people at Bramall Lane - yours truly included - knew anything more about Lys Mousset other than the fact he was pretty quick and powerful. After scoring his fifth goal since moving to South Yorkshire during the close season, it is fair to say the Frenchman is no mystery now. And that could pose a problem for United's hierarchy over the summer because, in this kind of form, Mousset is bound to attract admiring glances from what Wilder likes to describe as "big, powerful clubs."

LOWLIGHT
Another match, another farcical demonstration of VAR; a system supposedly so wonderful it was capable of bringing about world peace as well as spotting a handball in the penalty area or trip on the edge of the box.
Twice, referee David Coote saw decisions referred to Stockley Park. And on both occasions, first when Chris Basham was suspected of handling before Dean Henderson's challenge on a Wolves forward was also investigated, neither review was necessary. Unfortunately, the powers-that-be have invested so much - time, money and reputation - in this, we are stuck with it.

CHAPTER 8

Norwich City, 8th December

The events at the Lane last night have left me so frustrated. Thursday night football (for Amazon Prime) and we welcomed Newcastle. Before the game I was probably more nervous than any other game this season to date. If we win we go 11 points clear of the bottom 3.

What happened was crazy. We had so much of the ball but weren't quick enough and they camped out behind the ball. They got a goal out of nowhere and then the Norwich tactics from 2 years previous were then evident. The ref was such a mug, every time they faked injury he stopped play. Then in the second half the worst VAR situation yet. Linesman (yes that's what their called, although last night I had other words for him) flagged for what everyone in the ground thought was offside, Shelvey carried on and put the ball in the net. We all demanded he was booked but it went to VAR and to the horror of 29,000 Blades the goal was given. Yes play to the whistle but ffs any player who says they'd carry on

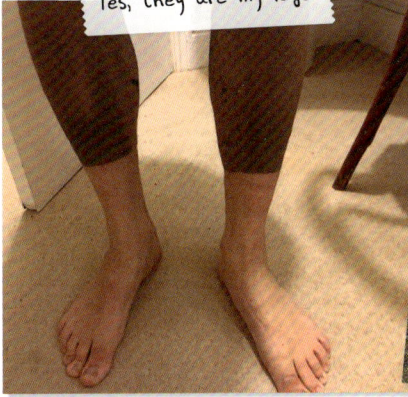
Yes, they are my legs!

playing when a flag is raised is a liar. Woke up still livid. Set off in the wind and yes you've guessed it, rain. Although it did get better. My morning thoughts consisted of VAR and politics. Due to this my average speed was well up on normal. It was a good ride overall. Met Mum and Dad for lunch at Newark. Love Newark, lovely memories nipping up and down the Trent to Local bars. Made it to the B&B in quick time, not the best place but welcoming, which is the most important thing. Either I've put a ridiculous amount of weight on or I've just showered in the smallest shower cubicle in the world. Anna and Jordan will be joining me later so sat here in towel watching Minder. Brings back some good memories. As we were in the middle of nowhere we went into Sleaford. Seemed a nice

place. Always nice to wear my Blades hat in a new town. Great to see people look over and give the thumbs up. Back to B&B and perhaps 4 too many Malts. Waking up I feel the Whiskies. Radio Sheffield had promised to call at 7.45am so I went outside to get a signal. Eventually got a call at five to. Now beginning to get really pissed off with having to self publish this. The presenter was more interested in finding out if I was doing it naked. No mention of who I'm raising funds for. Ignoring the disappointment of the call I set off in decent conditions. Having Anna & Jordan doing back up is really making things easier. No panniers is so much better. After only a few miles I hear my phone ping. Normally I'd leave it but something made me stop and look. Oh Jesus Christ, it was a message from Lia, telling me that Jan had passed away on their cycle trip through South America. I cycled across America with Jan and Lia a couple of years ago and have met up a couple of times since. We've all had those times when we've received such information but this was a real knife in my heart. A quality bloke, from Holland. A strong caring guy who I connected with. I stopped literally in the middle of nowhere to wipe my watering eyes. Life is such a shit sometimes. I had to pull myself together and concentrate. I ride for Jan today. Arriving in Swaffham I feel numb.

We go for a few beers and spread the Blade word. A couple of Norwich fans who had obviously had a couple of shandies were in one bar but I couldn't even be arsed to get involved with some banter. It's so much better having someone do back up, however, it has its draw backs, such as going to bed blowing bubbles with 30 miles to do on game day. Great night though.

I didn't really sleep well due to drinking Vodka and Red Bull. Felt a little delicate first thing and wondered how the short ride will feel. After the initial thoughts that the carrot man would pay me a visit I started feeling strong. I shed a few tears for Jan today, just can't believe he's gone. Met Anna and Jordan a few miles out to pull on my favourite shirt, wearing with pride. A few yells of 'go on Blade' as I enter Norwich. Amazing how the encouragement seems to reduce the pains. Arrive in good time to get the usual photo outside the ground.

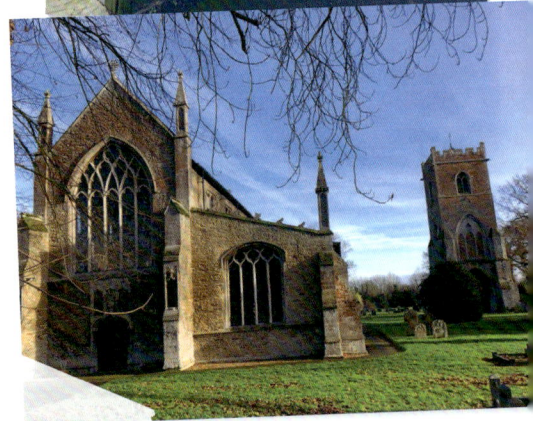

Changed in the car and then into the ground. Must have been here at least 6 times now. Remember the first time when we were in the third division and they were top of Division 1. An FA Cup match which we lost 3-2 but wow great game and thousands of Blades everywhere. Another time when Andy Cooper drove and we didn't arrive till half time. 2-0 up at the time we ended up drawing 2-2 with Fleckies uncle scoring for them in the last minute. Wish I had missed the first half today, poor performance. They were 1-0 up at half time. I make no excuse for thinking 'is this the start of a bad run' as we are Blades after all, however I should know better and keep my mouth shut, otherwise I will end up cycling everywhere, o hang on......

The second half was just brilliant. If I don't get chance to say it to you in person, thank you Chris Wilder. I know you get how we feel but seriously this is incredible. When Baldy scores our winner the guy behind me was drinking some whiskey from his hip flask, I had it thrown all over me, including my eyes. The journey home from the most isolated ground in the Premier League was a joy. Very mixed emotions with the devastating news about a good friend. The Children's Hospital have started getting on board, now we have momentum. I will do this and make some kids happier.

Daniel Farke and Chris Wilder on the touchline

Blades score huge win at Carrow Road

Long-distance 'derby' with Canaries full of twists and turns

JAMES SHIELD
The Star's Blades writer

Email: james.shield@jpimedia.co.uk
Twitter: @JamesShield1

Chris Wilder, jubilant at the victory

NORWICH	1
BLADES	2

First we had poor time-keeping.

Then, after Chris Wilder's wild celebrations following a win here angered Norwich City's supporters, Sheffield United's decision to redecorate Carrow Road's away dressing room because they objected to its bright pink paint job.

Now we can add another controversial episode to the list of incidents which has helped fuel one of football's most surprising rivalries. The red card that never was.

Or, as City manager Daniel Farke preferred to call it, the VAR "disaster". That was his take on the sight of visiting defender Chris Basham being sent-off and then ushered back onto the pitch following a review by Stockley Park.

"What I have learnt this season, is that every VAR overruled decision seems to go against us," Farke sighed, when asked about Basham's tackle on Kenny McLean. "It has been a disaster for us, and I don't know why. If it was not a red card, then we have to accept this.

"I have stopped complaining about this. Because I do not expected any VAR decision to go in our favour through the season."

Despite leading after goals from Enda Stevens and George Baldock had cancelled-out Alex Tettey's opener for the hosts, Wilder

The teams

Norwich City: Kruhl, Aarons, Byram (Lewis 72), Godfrey, Zimmermann, Vrancic (Srbeny 80), Hernandez (Cantwell 72), Buendia, Pukki, McLean, Tettey. Not used: Fahrmann, Stiepermann, Trybull, Amadou.
Sheffield United: Henderson, Basham, Egan, O'Connell, Stevens, Baldock, Norwood (Besic 66), Fleck, Lundstram, Mousset (Robinson 66), McGoldrick (McBurnie 83). Not used: Moore, L Freeman, Sharp, Jagielka.
Referee: Simon Hooper

Dean Henderson signals for a hand ball on Norwich's goal

acknowledged Basham's reprieve had spared his team the prospect of a nervous and potentially damaging 15 minutes at the end of the game.

"They were better than us first-half," Wilder said. "We went backwards and square. We didn't do the fundamentals. Then, second-half, we were Sheffield United."

It wasn't a derby. But it felt like one beforehand. Even though, in terms of geography, approach and even image, the two clubs are miles apart.

However, with much of the pre-match analysis focusing on the relationship between Chris Wilder and Daniel Farke, the significance of this game appeared to escape many people's notice.

There might have been 10 places between them ahead of kick-off. In terms of points, however, the gap was only eight.

Wilder, the Sheffield United manager, had reminded his team of that before they boarded their plane to Norfolk on Saturday evening.

Twenty-four hours earlier, when he played host to the media at the Steelphalt Academy training complex, most of those in attendance wanted to discuss 'Coach Gate', impromptu makeovers of Carrow Road's away dressing room or another of the seemingly endless series of spats which, by Wilder's admission, have given United's recent meetings with Norwich City "plenty of extra edge".

He played along, providing a few entertaining anecdotes and illuminating insights. But Wilder's sights remained fixed on trying to win a contest which, despite not being the highest profile fixture on either club's schedule, he suspected would go a long way towards shaping the rest of the campaign.

"If they get a result here," Wilder predicted, referring to the opposition, "Then they'll

fancy reeling in a few of those sides above them. And we're one of those."

It was a theory which explained his mood afterwards.

"That's an important win for us," Wilder said. "A very important win because, make no mistake, we know how good Norwich are. There were things we weren't pleased with. Particularly before the break and I think you can say that a few things were mentioned [during the interval].

"But then we really looked ourselves. Which we had to. Because everything you get, in this division especially, is just so important."

Despite describing City as the "best in the Championship by a long chalk last season", Wilder has watched his squad adapt quicker to life in the Premier League than the one they were promoted alongside.

Travelling south in ninth and beaten only once in eight outings, United's high-octane football and spiteful attitude has captured the imagination of supporters and fellow professionals alike. Both were conspicuous by the absence before the interval but returned, as goals from Enda Stevens and George Baldock cancelled out Alex Tettey's opener for City, with a vengeance after the break.

"I thought it was a dangerous game for us," Wilder said. "A real dangerous game for us, because of the familiarity of the two teams. I think it went under the radar how well both of our two teams did, because when you look at the money that has been spent elsewhere

in the division, we should have been nowhere near it."

Predictably, given the way their rivalry has developed of late, the 72nd competitive meeting between United and City spawned another controversial moment. It came, with around a quarter-of-an-hour remaining, when Chris Basham was sent-off for foul on Kenny McLean.

The United defender protested his innocence before being summoned back to Simon Hooper when VAR officials at Stockley Park instructed the referee to rescind his red card and issue a yellow one instead.

Publicly at least, Farke and Wilder agree on little. But with the latter later suggesting the

system should be scrapped, they were singing from the same hymn sheet in the press room afterwards.

"It sucks the life out of the stadium and out of the fans," Farke said, pausing for thought and taking a mighty deep breath. "Let me tell you, it also sucks the life out of the coach."

"I am a traditionalist. So maybe I could handle a few more mistakes if we can keep the emotion in the game."

"There were 28 or 29 thousand people in the stadium and they were all of the same opinion," Wilder said, echoing his counterpart's opinion. "I don't think the fans – and they are the real stakeholders in all of this – really want it do they."

2019-20 HOME KIT OUT NOW

Sheffield United

Chris Basham leads the celebrations after the game at Carrow Road

Enda Stevens scores United's first

George Baldock celebrates scoring United's second goal

Highlight

A fabulous second half revival ensured Sheffield United bounced back from defeat to maintain their unbeaten away form in the Premier League.

Two quick-fire second half goals from Enda Stevens and George Baldock helped Sheffield United win this crucially significant game between the two clubs who gained automatic promotion from the Championship last season.

Alex Tettey had fired Norwich City in front as Daniel Farke's side controlled the game before the break.

But United improved beyond all recognition after the interval, and got their reward when first Stevens and then his fellow wing-back, after providing the assist, pounced.

Lowlight

Unsurprisingly VAR features again, just as it did in defeat to Newcastle United on Thursday night, but this time it actually got the Blades out of a hole. Sheffield United got the benefit of the doubt on this occasion but Chris Wilder will be bitterly disappointed, after watching his team climb to eighth, that the post-match talk was once again all about VAR. United were leading 2-1 when Chris Basham received a straight red card for a foul on Kenny McLean.

But officials at Stockley Park told referee Simon Hooper to downgrade it to a yellow.

Both sets of supporters voiced their displeasure with the system at various stages of the contest.

Celebrating the first goal

CHAPTER 9

Brighton, 21st December

The one I've really been dreading. Since the Norwich game I've had a bad cold/sinus infection together with a horrid cough. I've tried to take it really easy but the symptoms haven't cleared up as I prepare to depart on a pea souper of a morning.

Mum and Dad are moving in as Kate (doggy Hotel) is away for Christmas. I set off really concerned that I won't make it. Trying to take it very easy I don't feel too bad initially. I try to stay positive but do eventually start to flag. The fog seems to take an age to clear. This can't be helping my cold. Trying to take my mind off things I play a game of room 101 relating to my day.

1. Young guys who think they are Billy big bollox driving the loudest cars possible. For their reference, when people look at you as you speed past they ain't saying 'wow isn't he great?' They're saying 'what a knob.'
2. Headwind. Happens virtually every time I ride.
3. Fog, miserable, horrid and no good to anyone.
4. Weather forecasters. When they say 'we're not quite sure what direction this low pressure will take so keep your eye out.' What's the point of you then?

Today seems the longest ride ever. The days of riding in sunny warm weather seems a lifetime ago. Still, it could be worse, it could be snowing. I arrive in the dark. The place is really nice. A quick whiskey to warm the cockles, hot shower, then a little lie down. FaceTime Dad and Lola comes into view, never thought I'd miss a dog as much as I do when on these trips. During the night I can hear the wind howling, yeah like that's

54

gonna be a northerly, NOT.

Decent nights sleep.

Duddington is a really lovely place and The Royal Oak is definitely on my list for the next trip down south. The ascent at the start of day 2 surprised me. Legs were feeling unusually tired. Actually enjoyed the ride for the majority of the way. Called at the same cafe in Papworth as I did for the Tottenham trip. Really smashing couple who deserve to do well.

Manage to make it to 15 from the B&B before the rain came. Prior to that the headwinds were horrendous, AGAIN! One day I will get a tailwind. Shortly after Royston (nice place) I seemed to be climbing forever. The route had indicated I'd be doing a total ascent of 2600ft, so why the fuck was I now on 2800ft with another 10 miles to go. Yes I was angry. A guy in a car shouted something, I asked 'what?' He said 'change to a higher gear' I was just spinning my legs, a) because I was shattered b) because I was struggling to get the chain into larger ring. 'How's fuck off sound?' Good job he didn't stop cos I was as weak as a kitten.

Finally made it and think it's reward time in the shape of a pint or 4.

Felt exhausted so got to bed early. Definitely not 100% and my mental health is at a low ebb. Checking my twitter page I see an emotional plea from Luke Prest, an old work colleague and fellow Blade. A flurry of donations take the total so far to £2000. Some words are so encouraging and all of sudden I feel a warm droplet of water fall down my cheek.

I was going to wait until it stopped raining but I would have missed the match so I turn the legs again and within 5 minutes my gear was as wet as if I'd got in the bath.

I was feeling a bit stronger and within no time I was cycling past White Hart Lane then was right in the middle of London.

Stopped on London Bridge to admire our Capital. We are lucky you know. I knew the route was going to be flattish until 35 miles from the end. The hills arrived with strong headwinds. This one is testing every ounce of Physical and Mental strength I have. I cycle through a ridiculous amount of flood water. As I get closer to the evenings destination of East Grinstead I'm really taken with the area. Really nice part of England. Arriving at the nice Crowne Plaza the usual 'modern' room awaits with no bleeding radiators ffs. How on earth am I going to dry my gear? I phone reception to see if they can help but was told they couldn't. I said that's

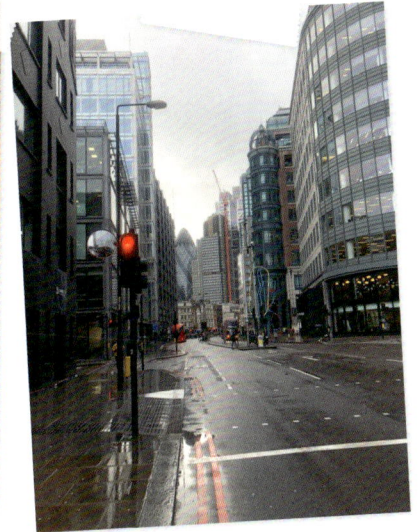

fine, will mention in my Tripadvisor review. Within 2 mins they phoned back saying 'we forgot, we have a big dryer.' Argh well we got there in the end. Well I thought we had got there in the end, my socks and under thermal vest hadn't turned up. So the staff say they can't have gone out of the laundry room. Therefore the guy on laundry is now listing a couple of items on eBay and there's nowt I can do about it. Ditching climb didn't disappoint and as I reached the summit the rain was bloody ridiculous. I kid you not I just started laughing out loud at the horrendous conditions and shouted 'TAKE ME NOW LORD' Eventually made it. Nice looking ground and really decent people.

If I wasn't as exhausted I would have spent longer chatting to a few Brighton fans who had become my new Bessie's. I enter the ground early and take a little time out sat in the stadium before anyone else appears. 4 years ago (when I made this promise) If someone would have said that the Blades would be top 10 and you would have cycled to all away games up to Christmas, I would have called for help. I'm actually feeling numb, comfortably numb.

Chatting to Sarah, new friend, via Paul Shields prior to the match I said what I've said before every away match to date this season 'I have a bad feeling about this one'. It's important that us Blades continue with this attitude because I would hate to ever become Billy Big Bollox like your Liverpool's and Man City's. Congrats by the way to Liverpool on winning club world Championship. The Blades start 'on the front foot' a beautiful Wilder ism. Always 'leave through front door'

After only a few minutes we score from a cross. As we've been pissed off in recent weeks with VAR my celebrations are muted. Rightly so as another one is ruled against us. Not long after, he's our striker, he's our number 9 battles with their two centre halves and shoots hard and into the corner of the net. This one we celebrate. Literally bodies flying everywhere. I seriously haven't ever seen so many drunk people in my life. I'm not kidding you some guys looked that drunk they looked like zombies.

In the second half I tell (didn't ask) a steward that I'm sitting in the disabled section. When asked why I simply said cos I'm knackered and sick of bodies falling on me. We see out the game, we should have been well out of sight to be honest. Every Blade is desperate for Didsy to score. Another great chance missed. Jeeez when he scores we will go crazy. Yet another VAR decision goes against us. Correct though.

Quickly dash round to where I locked the bike. Get chatting to a Brighton fan and cycle a short way with him. One thing (and hope I'm not speaking too soon) I've found is I've not once felt threatened by any opposition fan. 35 years ago my bike and me with it would be in various pieces. The 4 mile ride to the station was again in torrential rain. FFS my nice dry clothes were soaking. The train journey was incredibly slow to London. Loads of Blades on the train, one sat next to me started quizzing me about my adventures. They then gave me what they had towards the fundraising. The whole carriage then came up one by one handing over fivers, tenners and even twenty pound notes. I felt embarrassed to be honest but humbled nevertheless.

Due to the floods the train was going the pace of a Blade on a Bike, and let me tell you that's slow. Only just make connection at St Pancras or as one of the young slightly drunk Blades next to me said St Pancreas. Very sad to hear the passing of Martin Peters. Played and managed the Blades for a short spell in 81. Not our best period but I understand he was a really nice guy. RIP.

So so pleased to see Anna meet me off the train. When I get home, my Lola is so pleased to see me. Happy Christmas everyone and UTB.

Golden hour of hard work proves a point about front man

JAMES SHIELD
The Star's Blades writer
Email: james.shield@jpimedia.co.uk
Twitter: @JamesShield1

Oli McBurnie celebrates his goal for Sheffield United against Brighton

Winner was perfect goal for McBurnie

BRIGTON	0
UNITED	1

In a sense, it was the perfect Oli McBurnie goal.

Clinical, ever so slightly scruffy and all about sheer, bloody-minded persistence.

That his third of the Premier League season also proved enough to secure this victory over Brighton and Hove Albion – a result which ensured Sheffield United remain unbeaten on the road since January – was a even more fitting tribute to a player who, despite making a steady but despite making a steady but unspectacular start to life with Chris Wilder's side, had earned himself a recall thanks to some tenacious displays during training.

You got the impression that United's manager felt Saturday's match was made for his record signing.

United had already seen an effort disallowed by VAR – John Egan adjudged to have handled as he turned the ball home – before the 23-year-old, socks down, shirt out and unshaven – hunted down Dean Henderson's clearance, held off two defenders and, refusing to dive despite being hustled by Lewis Dunk, beat Matthew Ryan.

Neal Maupay also had an attempted overturned by the video official, after Martin Montoya had strayed offside. But United, who finished the contest

The teams

Brighton: Ryan, Dunk, Stephens, Maupay, Trossard (Murray 46), Gross (Connolly 46), Webster, Mooy, Montoya (Bissouma 55), Propper, Burn. Not used: Button, Duffy, Bernardo, Alzate.

Sheffield United: Henderson, Baldock, Stevens, Basham, Egan, O'Connell, Norwood (Besic 83), L Freeman (Osborn 53), Lundstram, McGoldrick, McBurnie (Mousset 65). Not used: Verrips, Sharp, Robinson, Jagielka.

John Egan celebrates his goal before it was ruled out

only a point behind fourth-place, were the dominant force for long periods with David McGoldrick and substitute Lys Mousset later going close.

Jack O'Connell also thought he had doubled their lead, after pouncing upon Ryan's fumble. But Michael Oliver, overseeing operations at Stockley Park, intervened again.

Sixty-three minutes into this intriguing contest, and around 40 after scoring for the third time since joining Sheffield United, Oli McBurnie glanced towards the touchline and saw his number being displayed on the fourth official's electronic board.

After lolloping off the pitch, sharing a hug with Chris Wilder and then a fist-bump with another member of the visitors' coaching staff, the centre-forward climbed a couple of steps towards the back of the dug-out and collapsed, barely able to move, in one of its huge padded seats.

It was a revealing end to what proved a match-winning shift at Brighton and Hove Albion. A lung-busting hour containing countless runs, numerous challenges and one clinical finish.

Or, to put it another way, a display which reminded why his manager believes McBurnie and United are a perfect fit.

"It was a touch disappointing in terms of how we were with the ball," Wilder, who is prone to pick apart United's performances whenever they triumph, said. "We weren't at our best in terms of possession or momentum, I didn't think.

"People talk about the game, playing in between the lines and all this lovely other stuff. But there has to be something else to it as well, especially when you are a team like us."

What that means, as Wilder has reminded on countless occasions, is a squad which

has to work hard for every point it gets.

And with 28 in the bag already, his players are clearly prepared to work ridiculously hard. And none more so than McBurnie who, despite making a steady but unspectacular start to his United career, has proven willing to muck in, chase lost causes and basically sacrifice himself for others.

His effort at the AMEX Stadium, which saw Wilder's side end the contest within touching distance of fourth, was a reward for those long afternoons he spent clattering into defenders at places like Everton and Watford, who make the journey north on Boxing Day.

United might have secured positive results against both. But McBurnie, despite putting his body on the line, received precious little recognition afterwards.

Signed from Swansea City during the close season, where he excelled under Wilder's opposite number Graham Potter, the 23-year-old had another reason to feel vindicated by his performance in Sussex. Spearheading Albion's attack was Neal Maupay, a player United had tried to recruit after waving goodbye to the Championship but who chose to swap Brentford for the south coast instead.

Having entered Saturday's game searching for his fourth goal in five outings, the Frenchman would have been an excellent addition to Bramall Lane's ranks. He had an effort disallowed for offside

following McBurnie's intervention. But, a peripheral figure for much of the fixture, it was impossible to escape the conclusion that the latter is better-suited to United at this stage of their top-flight development.

"Oli is a talented boy. He scored a load of goals in a very technical side last year," Wilder said. "It's difficult when chances are at a premium, which they always are at this level. We could have done with the second one."

Although that did not arrive United deserved to prevail over opponents coached by the man responsible for masterminding their last defeat on the road.

Potter later admitted as much himself and, perhaps inadvertently, provided a revealing insight into why, since McBurnie's strike for City 11 months ago, they travel to Manchester City later this month hoping to equal a record. I

t was during the 1947/48 campaign, when Burnley prevailed 1-0 at Huddersfield, that a newly promoted club avoided losing any of its first 10 away outings at the highest level.

"Because they can attack quite direct, because they can go down the sides and also overload you," Potter reflected. "It creates a feeling of stress."

Brighton and Hove Albion's Neal Maupay was wanted by Sheffield United

Sheffield United

Oli McBurnie scored his third Premier League goal for Sheffield United against Brighton and Hove Albion

Oli McBurnie fires home for Sheffield United at the AMEX Stadium

Sheffield United's George Baldock tackles Lewis Dunk of Brighton

Highlight

It was a big call to make. But United have a habit of making bold but ultimately successful calls so perhaps it was no surprise when Oli McBurnie, preferred in attack to leading goalscorer Lys Mousset, emerged as the match winner. McBurnie, United's record signing in the transfer market, was responsible for the finish which last saw Chris Wilder's side beaten away from home. The former Swansea City centre-forward, whose effort at the Liberty Stadium propelled Graham Potter's side to a narrow victory in South Wales, returned to haunt his former manager at The Amex Stadium with another well-taken finish. Potter admitted he did not hold a grudge against McBurnie after watching him help United put Brighton to the sword.

Lowlight

Poor David McGoldrick. The United centre-forward returned home from Sussex still without a Premier League goal to his name this season after missing a gilt-edged chance during the second-half of the win over Albion. After latching onto Ben Osborn's pass and then rounding the goalkeeper, McGoldrick appeared odds on the score in front of the United fans. But rather than finding the back of the net, he could only find the outside of the near post instead. McGoldrick impressed throughout. But his reaction to that miss - despite hearing the away supporters chant his name immediately afterwards - suggested he is growing increasingly frustrated by his failure - so far at least - to convert opportunities.

Jack O'Connell of Sheffield United at the AMEX Stadium

CHAPTER 10

Man City, 29th December

Was looking forward to getting going. Love Christmas but equally love getting house straight after Boxing Day and back to normal.

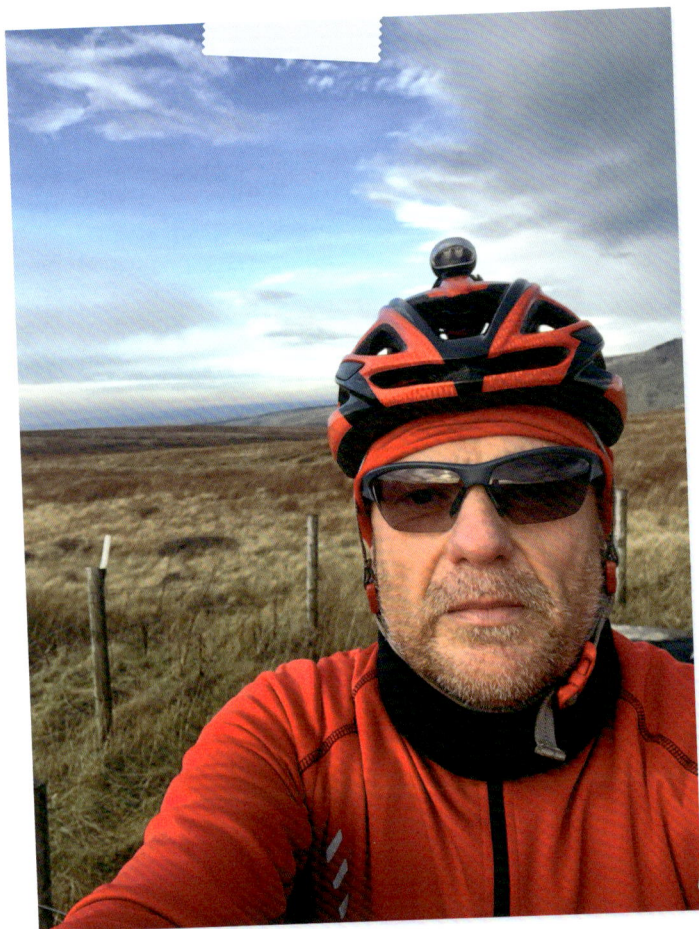

The Weather Forecast first thing 'Southerly winds, mild' so why the hell was the wind in my face when I'm heading West? My mate, Bob had kindly taken my bag before Christmas so I could ride on road bike, so much easier. A young guy, Chris who's doing a Journalist course Media Production at Hillsborough College contacted me a few weeks ago asking if he could do a video of my venture. He chose this as a good one to take footage of me riding. Tried to tuck my belly in when I saw him. The ride was slow (could feel the extra pounds) but enjoyable. At the top of the Snake I paused, I'm half way, 91/2 matches.

Didn't judge timings as I arrived within a couple of miles of the ground with 5 hours to kick off. Stopped at pub for yet another Turkey dinner.

Got to ground and waited for Bob. My concerns at getting in the ground with my bag, thankfully were eased after showing the security guys the contents – my helmet and bike shoes. Fellow Blades were fantastic, offering their cars or coaches as storage. The Blades fans have been tremendous to date. Chris Wilders team selection was genius. It would have worked if VAR and the ref hadn't have had their say, AGAIN. So a new feeling, leaving an away game defeated. Not too despondent at all. I go again in 3 days. Get a decent train back although train has the usual young fools who can't take their shandy.

Oliver Norwood shakes hands with Blades old boy Kyle Walker

Lady luck absent once more as Pep lavishes praise on the Blades

JAMES SHIELD
The Star's Blades writer

Email: james.shield@jpimedia.co.uk
Twitter: @JamesShield1

Unbeaten run ends in real controversy

MANCHESTER CITY 2
SHEFFIELD UNITED 0

After 18 matches, 344 days and nine top-flight battles against some of the richest clubs in the business, Sheffield United's long unbeaten run away from home came to an end at the home of the reigning Premier League champions.

But referee Chris Kavanagh and Stuart Attwell, overseeing this fixture in the VAR suite at Stockley Park, exerted greater influence over the final outcome than any of the star-studded names in Manchester City's line-up; including goalscorers Sergio Aguero and Kevin de Bruyne.

Attwell made his presence felt when, with the contest still evenly poised, he ruled Lys Mousset had strayed into an offside position before converting a sumptuous John Fleck pass. Then it was Kavanagh's turn to intervene, impeding the Scot as he prepared to receive possession and setting in motion the chain of events which saw Aguero break the deadlock.

With United posing more questions than they were being forced to answer themselves, Pep Guardiola admitted "it would have been very difficult to win" had Mousset's effort been allowed to stand. Although City produced the occasional moment of brilliance, United were the more creative force in the game when

The teams

Manchester City: Bravo, Walker, Sterling (Jesus 88), Aguero (Foden 81), Zinchenko, Rodrigo, De Bruyne, Silva (Gundogan 63), Fernandinho, Mahrez, Garcia. Not used: Carson, Mendy, Cancelo, Otamendi.
Sheffield United: Henderson, Basham, Egan, O'Connell, Stevens, Baldock, Norwood, Fleck, Besic (McBurnie 76), Robinson (McGoldrick 60), Mousset. Not used: Verrips, L Freeman, Sharp, Jagielka, Osborn.
Referee: Chris Kavanagh

Fernandinho of Manchester City and Billy Sharp

Mousset, recalled in attack alongside Callum Robinson, profited from Fleck's perfectly weighted and flighted assist across the hosts' rearguard. The decision to disallow the Frenchman's effort was questionable. And so, much to United's frustration, was the one to allow Aguero's opener to stand after Kavanagh had obstructed Fleck.

A little over 48 hours before kick-off, when he sat down with the media to discuss Sheffield United's forthcoming visit to Manchester City, Chris Wilder made no secret of his admiration for the manager he would soon be meeting inside the Etihad Stadium's technical area.

"He's changed the game," Wilder said, when the conversation turned towards Pep Guadiola. "And not many managers can claim to have done that in the history of football."

The former Barcelona, Brescia and Roma midfielder has transformed touchline attire too. But it is Guardiola's tactical nous, not his Stone Island jacket or Dsquared2 jeans, which have earned Wilder's respect since his arrival in England three years ago. The passing, the movement and the constant rotation - three hallmarks of the Catalan's teams - were all in evidence during both clubs' final Premier League fixture of 2019.

Likewise the suffocating pressure applied to the opposition whenever they dared to wrestle possession away from Kevin De Bruyne, Riyad Mahrez and Sergio Aguero.

Although the battle of wits between the respective benches was fascinating - United, mindful of City's preference for playing high up the pitch, selecting the turbo-charged Callum Robinson and Lys Mousset at centre-forward - this result was ultimately decided by someone 197 miles away in a glass

fronted building on a nondescript industrial estate.

Predictably, understandably, that angered Wilder who after initially pledging to give video reviews a chance, is now sick of talking about them.

"Just hit 'play' because I've already made my thoughts clear," he replied, when quizzed on Mousset's disallowed 'goal'. "Do we want people drawing silly lines all over the place? Do we want people putting blurred lines on things that no one else can understand? No. But that's what we have got."

Wilder then turned his attention to events which, before De Bruyne applied the coup-de-grace, put City on course to victory.

"He's definitely affected things," Wilder said, describing the moment referee Chris Kavanagh obstructed John Fleck and in turn allowed Aguero to break the deadlock. "In fairness, he (Kavanagh) invited me into his room afterwards and was very open about it. It was a private conversation.

"Whether or not the PGMOL issue a statement, we'll have to see. I'll keep things private but you can put two and two together. Let's leave it at that."

Despite the gulf between them in terms of top-flight experience and of course financial resources, United looked more than City's equals for much of this game. The finest move of the first-half, possibly even the match, was crafted by two midfielders wearing red and white stripes

Sheffield United players applaud their fans at the Etihad

as first Oliver Norwood and then John Fleck, demonstrating a much better grasp of geometry than the officials at Stockley Park, sent Mousset bearing down on City's penalty area. His shot was on target. Claudio Bravo, deputising for the suspended Ederson, powerless to prevent it reaching the back of the net. But Stuart Attwell, from the safety of his bunker in London's south-western suburbs, ruled Mousset had strayed offside.

It was a dubious call. But nowhere near as controversial as the one which allowed Aguero to break the deadlock. As he prepared to receive Norwood's pass, Fleck was impeded by Kavanagh

and surrendered possession. Aguero's finished in the manner you would expect of a marksman who reputedly earns around £250,000 a week. But United were incredulous, actually make that downright furious, that after studying a replay Attwell allowed this goal to stand.

"If he hadn't been offside," Guardiola said, scrolling back to Mousset's run, "then it would have been incredibly difficult to beat them."

"I already knew it but now I really understand," he continued, "why Sheffield are in the position they are in the table."

United's performance, as Guardiola appeared to concede, deserved better.

Sheffield United

Oliver Norwood leads the complaints to referee Chris Kavanagh that he got in the way, changing an attacking option into a fatal defensive one for the Blades

Billy Sharp of Sheffield Utd directs a header that hit the post. Pics Simon Bellis/Sportimage

George Baldock is challenged by Manchester City's Alexander Zinchenko

Highlight

The fact that Lys Mousset broke through the defence of the reigning Premier League champions shows United's attacking class.

Mousset had managed to put on the pressure even before VAR ruled his goal offside when early on he got close enough to get in a header, but sent it wide.

And the Blades' £10 million signing also put one into the side netting.

The fact that Mo Besic and Billy Sharp also troubled the City goal highlights the Blades' ability to put pressure on some of the best defences money can buy.

City manager Pep Guardiola said he was all too aware of the Untied's strengths. "They are good in the long balls, defending.

"It's not a secret where they are in the table," he said of the newly-promoted Blades.

Lowlight

The combined intervention of the referee's body and another armpit-offside VAR adjudication cost the Blades dear.

Fans and pundits alike have been scathing about VAR damaging the game.

This week saw Lys Mousset's early goal ruled out, which would have given United the lead.

Then referee Chris Kavanagh managed to block the Blades defence long enough for Aguero to put City 1-0 up.

Chris Wilder is not claiming United would have won had the incidents gone in his team's favour, but he is sure the game's momentum changed.

"I am not saying we would have won the game, or got a result, but it changes the game," said Wilder.

Chris Wilder waves to the Blades fans

CHAPTER 11

Liverpool, 2nd January

Happy New Year one and all.
When the powers that be changed this fixture date I thought it best
to spread it over 2 days even though I have done Liverpool in a day
but thought on the side of caution allowing for snow.

As it was only 45 miles today I set off later. Dropped Lola off at Kate's via police station to try and get them to shift a weed smoker from outside my house. How the hell doesn't Dronfield have a manned police station? 25,000 population with no police station, madness. So as I set off my mood was already edging towards Mr Angry. Roads were quiet as expected which was nice. A bit hilly today but took my time. As I drifted into cycle zone out mode I started playing at Praise or Grumble. Praise – start with a good one, the Weather. Yes a tad cold but it is Winter and it could be a lot worse. Grumble – some cyclists. Yes I'm one but when the minority ride 2 or sometimes 3 abreast it drives me mad Yes The Highway Code allows for such behaviour but everyone also knows it winds drivers up. Another one for my friends on 2 wheels. When ever I ride I ensure I wear bright colours for obvious reasons. Why o why do some cyclists ride dressed as roads? I kid you not I saw 1 guy today in all black with a white line down his back! Talk about asking for trouble. Grumble – twats who think it's ok to chuck litter out their cars. FFS why do this especially in the Peak District. Grumble – Me! What is wrong with me. Cycling down towards Calver crossroads a car passes me with the letters 'owls' on his number plate. I shout out

'Wanker' why do that, not nice. New Years Resolution 'be nicer to our South Barnsley friends' see I can't help myself.

First night away match of the season. Arrive at Anfield after a nice ride. Yes Tottenhams ground is fantastic but there is definitely something to be said for proper football grounds. I put Anfield in this bracket, its brick clad exterior with clean lines to me is how I'd like to see the Lane developed. I seem to remember that pre redevelopment of their main stand it was really tight with houses right upto the rear. A steward confirmed to me that they had purchased 3 streets to facilitate the new stand extension. If I get chance to sit down with the powers that be at the club I will show them my sketches.

Phase 1 - build a new kop behind the existing one, 15k capacity. Brilliant facilities required for Shreds army.

Phase 2 - build a new South Stand behind existing one, double tier so prawn sandwich lot can have boxes.

Phase 3 and 4 - there's more room now for John Street and Bramall Lane. May cost a quid or two but 45,000 stadium with extra facilities will match the management and team we have.

The stewards were on duty early at Anfield. I arrived at 12pm and bearing in mind the game kicks off at 8pm I was amazed at the number of people about. Cycling back into the centre of Liverpool a car horn was going furiously at me. What the hell, then a scouser shouting 'alright mate? You're the guy who's riding for charity yeah' I gave him the thumbs up and he's like going crazy 'oh brilliant man brilliant', made my day. Had a very lazy afternoon indeed. Laid on bed and just did nothing. Very rare I do that. I'm undecided whether to have a beer or not. It took me all of 10 seconds when I got to the bar to decide on a Becks. The Hotel is full of Liverpool fans but not from Liverpool. Irish, Spanish, German even Americans in attendance. Made me realise we are going toe to toe with probably one of the biggest clubs in the world. A far cry from Shrewsbury or Yeovil. This situation (sat in Hotel Bar full of Liverpool fans) makes me realise how naughty I am. I couldn't resist but take my jumper off exposing my blades shirt. To be fair as most if not all were Johnny Foreigners they don't bat an eyelid. Arriving at the ground by bus I realise how ridiculously ahead Liverpool are from not just us but most clubs. It's 6pm and 2 hours before kick off and the area around the ground is packed. Walking round to the Anfield Road end I arrive in time to see the Blades coach go past. 'Go on Blades' I shout. Not my wisest move as the other few thousand gathered

weren't impressed. I quickly walk upto the fan zone. Looked more like Sheffield Market. So now, I'm in the ground an hour and a half before kick off. Blades fans sang throughout. To be fair sometimes you have to accept you're up against the best club side in the world. Yes we weren't at our best but jeez they are good. We were never allowed to get it going and when we looked like breaking they were like snakes. Still 8th after playing Liverpool twice and City, we would all take that last August.

Bus back to centre and have a pint with some German guys. I tell them to spread the Sheff Utd word. Alarm set early to phone mum and wish her well for knee op.

Train home. Arriving at Lime street at 8.30am I realised it would stop at Chesterfield so had a sliding doors decision. Get off at Sheffield and ride home or Chesterfield. Decided as it was nice I'd get off at Sheffield. Mmm as it turned out it was the wrong decision. Coming past Radio Sheffield I stopped at the junction with St Mary's Gate. Waited for the green light then set off. Well I did but my bike didn't. The front wheel lodged in a road gully and I did a hand stand over the handle bars. Blood everywhere but I wasn't badly injured however my 10 year old favourite bike (Specialized Tri Cross) was finally a write off. The

bars were bent as was the front wheel. I
was gutted. This bike has took me on many
a mile, I guess at 10,000 miles in all.
Managed to crawl home. Off to JE
James to try find another trusty friend.
A visit from FC Fylde in the FA Cup
was a nice distraction from the league
and Chris Wilders decision to rest all
11 was spot on. Although Deano and
Bash were used perhaps not planned.
Just scrapped through, perhaps the
2-1 score line didn't reflect the game.
We should have been out of sight.
A 4th round trip to Millwall is our reward,
really? Wouldn't call it a reward but will
enjoy the trip on the train rather than bike.
A Friday visit from West Ham brought many
emotion. The fantastic news that Chris Wilder
has signed a new contract gives us a huge
lift. The first half was slow but second half
we got into them and caused them issues.
Again we should have been out of sight when
they thought they'd scored the equaliser.
Bloody Snodgrass again, ffs. The guys next
to me got up and left in a huff, hope they
saw the VAR verdict from the concourse.
It was like scoring a goal. The first VAR to
go with us. Wonder where we would be in
the league without VAR, 4th is my guess.
Made me laugh listening to TalkSPORT after
the match. 'It's wrong' 'It needs throwing out'

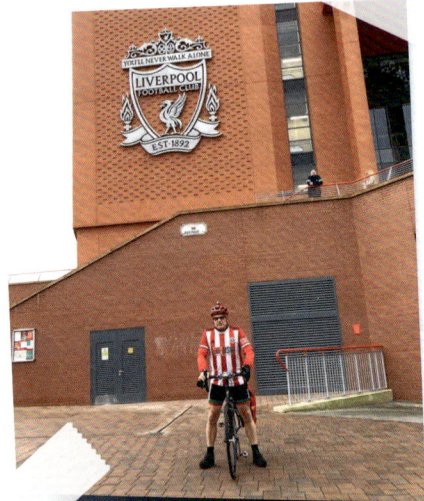

Funny I thought, a London club gets it go against them and it's all we hear. To be fair we would be equally frustrated, and have been. Preparing for the Arsenal trip, guess what the forecast is....... Storm force southerly winds, great this will be fun.

As touched on earlier a young student, Chris has been doing a short video on my story. He released it this week and it looks brilliant. Hope he gets a 2:1 whatever that means. On the back of this Alan Biggs got in touch via Twitter and invited me to join him on his Sheffield Live show. I was delighted to be able to advertise the JustGiving link. There also was Peter Elliot who is a really nice fella, very unassuming to say what he's achieved. Alan also a really nice guy and excellent at what he does. Pleased he helped me get the main message across which was trying to raise as much as possible for the Children's Hospital. We touched on my issues I've had with mental illness. A year ago I had a major breakdown. I knew at the time I shouldn't be putting on my family but I was in such a dark place. I really want to help others who suffer now I'm in a much better place. Exercise, although not the complete answer has helped me no end.

Reds prove their class after shutting down Blades

James Shield
james.shield@jpimedia.co.uk
@JamesShield1

Earlier in the day, before going into battle against the reigning European champions and Premier League title winners elect, Sheffield United's players were filmed trying to hold a training session in Stanley Park whilst shoo'ing a runaway pooch away from their improvised pitch.

The clip, which inevitably went viral on social media, highlighted the gulf in stature between two clubs at different stages of their footballing development. And yet, as Liverpool manager Jurgen Klopp later confirmed in his official programme notes, they also boast plenty in common. Culturally, tactically and personality-wise too.

"They strike me as a group who cares not one bit about what people outside of their circle think of them," the German, whose players are used to the best of everything, said. "I love this."

It isn't just United's attitude which has piqued Klopp's interest. He loves their style and staff too.

"There is nothing I could write here that would appropriately reflect what Chris and his team have achieved over the past few seasons," the 52-year-old continued. "I read a lot about their determination and fight. But this does them a disservice. They are smart in every department and this clearly comes from the manager."

Unfortunately for United, Klopp's welcome did not extend to the pitch where the hosts gave them precious little encouragement during 90 testing minutes.

But his words did reveal the depth of Liverpool's respect for the visitors from South Yorkshire who, by Klopp's own admission, had set their "toughest" test of the season so far at Bramall Lane in September.

It was after that contest when the two men in the technical area cemented their friendship. An hour after Georginio Wijnaldum's fortuitous strike towards the end of the second condemned United to defeat, Wilder and his opposite number could still be found talking football and plenty more besides over beer and the remnants of a post-match buffet pilfered from the home dressing room.

Some details of that conversation have since crept into the media, with Wilder providing a few extra morsels during the build-up to this fixture.

"I actually think the two cities have got plenty in common," he said. "Two teams, a big rivalry and, like them, we can turn out some damn good bands as well."

In a sense, although Sheffield's status as the birthplace of the modern game remains one of its best kept secrets, the trip to Anfield represented a glimpse into the future for United. Providing, of course, they can establish themselves at the highest level and then continue to progress.

With 76 major honours, including the FIFA World Club crown they secured towards the end of last month, Liverpool a profile few others can match.

But there is no reason, with a little imagination, ambition and help from regional politicians, why Wilder's employers can not achieve something similar, albeit on a more modest scale.

United might not have the trophies. But they do possess the history, the home and the heritage to become a "bucket list" destination for students of the sport. And also music too.

Those fans in the away end chanting "We support our local team" midway through the first-half might not thank anyone for saying so. And yes, they are right, identity is important.

But the tourists from across the globe, who began flooding into Liverpool as early as Wednesday night, help Klopp acquire players like Mo Salah and Virgil van Dijk. They produced the two most important touches of the first-half before Sadio Mane ended United's hopes of a comeback.

Dean Henderson, whose error had helped gift Liverpool a win four months ago, was hugely impressive on this occasion. Indeed, there were moments when it appeared he was taking part in a personal duel with Salah, whose 14th of the campaign laid the foundations for a win which moves Klopp's men 13 points clear at the top of the table.

But, before acrobatically tipping a long range shot from the Egyptian over the crossbar and turning another attempt past the foot of the post, Henderson was powerless to prevent Salah turning home from close range after a slip by George Baldock, who lost his footing at the vital moment, granted Andy Robertson both the time and the space to produce an inch-perfect cross.

Chasing shadows for the most part, as Liverpool pinged passes across the pitch, United would nevertheless almost certainly have equalised after John Fleck had punched a hole through the red wall in midfield, had van Dijk not whipped the ball away from Lys Mousset's feet.

Mane ensured Liverpool's unbeaten start remained intact when he turned home after the break; Henderson saving the Senegalese's initial effort following an exchange with Salah.

Substitute Oli McBurnie was inches away with connecting with a Jack O'Connell centre as the final whistle approached. But, in truth, the difference between the two sides was as stark as their choice of training facilities.

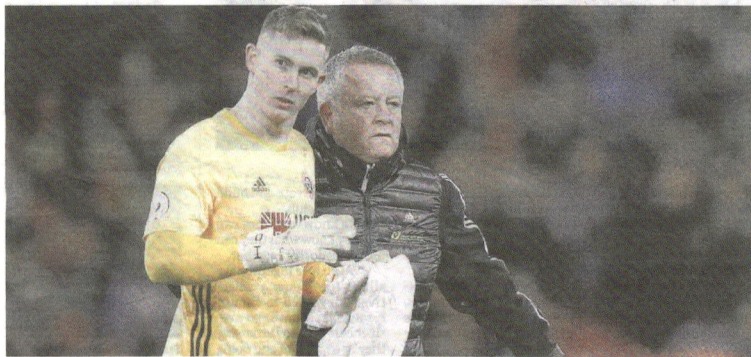

Liverpool's Virgil van Dijk keeps the United attack at bay.

Chris Wilder paid tribute to goalkeeper Dean Henderson for keeping United in the game. Picture: Sportimage

United well beaten on tough night at Anfield

Four months ago, when they last locked horns with Liverpool across the Pennines at Bramall Lane, Sheffield United argued with plenty of justification that the scoreline did not reflect their contribution to the game.

Ninety-six days later, after failing to gain revenge for that 1-0 defeat, neither Chris Wilder nor his side could have no such complaints. Indeed, as the visitors' manager admitted afterwards, it was Jurgen Klopp who probably felt short-changed by the final result.

The Premier League leaders, now 13 points clear at the top of the table and unbeaten in the competition for a year, were infinitely more superior than the 2-0 outcome would suggest.

"From our perspective, I was really disappointed," Wilder conceded. "I didn't think we laid a glove on them and the result, the 2-0, probably flattered us.

"If there was ever an example, of why they are world champions, European champions and soon to be champions of England, we saw it out there. People can talk about academies, rotations and all of that.

"But they won headers, tackles and races. And they won them better than us."

Liverpool: Alisson, van Dijk, Wijnaldum, Keita, Firmino, Mane (Origi 78), Salah (Elliott 90), Gomez, Henderson, Robertson (Lallana 89), Alexander-Arnold. *Not used:* Adrian, Milner, Phillips, Jones.

Sheffield United: Henderson, Baldock, Stevens, Basham, Egan, O'Connell, Norwood (Besic 78), Fleck, Lundstram, Mousset (McBurnie 66), McGoldrick (Sharp 66). *Not used:* Verrips, Robinson, Jagielka, Osborn.

George Baldock and his team-mates looking dejected at the end of the game Picture: Sportimage

Liverpool manager Jurgen Klopp applauds the fans at Anfield

CHAPTER 12

Arsenal, 18th January

Pleased my cycling buddy, Alex was joining me today for a few miles. First outing for my new grod. Felt heavy and was kicking myself for not changing tyres to 28's instead of 32.

On the way to Alex's at Brimington I went under the roundabout near JE James. I've thought this before about the tactile paving at the bottom of the ramps but today I nearly came off. The ribs are the wrong way. Need to chat with British Cycling. Weather to start wasn't too bad, no rain and just a gentle breeze. It was good to have Alex ride with me, seems to go quicker. Soon at 30 miles where we stopped for tea and crumpets. Said my farewells to Alex although was concerned he would manage to find his way home. Not known for his sense of direction is our Alex. Felt strong but then at 40 miles the wind started gathering pace. At the bottom of the days toughest hill the headwind was really strong and it started raining. ANYTHING ELSE LORD? I shouted out loud. Just then what can only be described as a matchstick on a bike went flying past me. Yes he was on a road bike and I'm on a tourer with Panniers but it was a watershed moment for me. Yes I'm able to ride all day but if I lost some timber it would be so much easier. Trouble is I'm so bloody greedy. Determined though that come May I will be 121/2 stone. Climbing the hill I was really struggling. Felt a major wall coming on. Had some protein bar but was still struggling in the now gusting winds. Stopped at a shop and bought a Marathon, o sorry, Snickers. Did help a little.

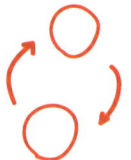

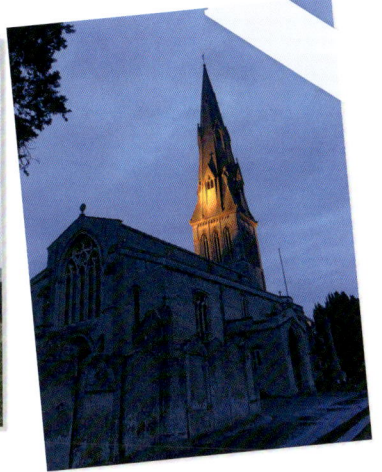

The afternoon was a slow slog as I went into cycle zone out. My brain started having a row with my legs, 'come on you lazy twats, move' 'fuck off knob head' came their reply. Was counting the miles down. The wind was just constantly in my face. At one point I actually thought I might cycle the other way for a mile to just have a tailwind.

It's rare I have an energy gel but was glad of it today.

Ten miles out had to turn the lights on. Arrived in the dark! That was really really tough.

Day 2. Looked out of the window and actually saw a hint of blue sky. It was lovely when I set off. Clear skies albeit still a headwind but not as bad as yesterday. Unbelievably I felt strong. The legs and brain had made up and were working together. In no time at all I stopped at the usual cafe (The Courtyard) in Papworth. I actually feel like a local in there now and will miss it. I noticed as I made light work of the Leek and Potato soup that rain had started falling. No worries I thought, the weather guys said showers.

Dear Weather guys

To normal people a shower is say 5 minutes long NOT 2 hours ffs. Drenched through all layers.

Eventually it stopped. I slightly changed the route which took me on the A10 a bit. Will be looking at that for the Palace trip, 60mph is National Speed Limit on single carriageway. I know that you see from my recent speed awareness course. I don't think there was one car doing less than 80.

Felt strong till the end of the ride today and finished crazy early compared to yesterday. Maybe a couple of shandies.......

I don't really think I have a strong northern accent but waiting to get served at the bar a guy said 'wouldn't put up with this up north pal'. Had a couple of beers with said guy who it turns out was a Spurs fan so wished me well for tomorrow. Really have had everything weather wise on this trip. Wind, rain and now ice. However it's a beautiful morning and as I've only 23 to do today no need for an early start. The sun rises and I'm actually really enjoying the morning sun. For the third time in recent weeks I cycle past White Hart Lane. Stop for a cuppa to kill time then complete the remaining 4 miles. Strange sort of location the Emirates. From memory it's built on an old gas works. All access is via bridges. Last time I came here was with Tom to watch them v Fulham. That day it was 3-3, great game. Ironically Arteta missed a last minute penalty for Arsenal that day. Met Paul Shields and his son Billy. Richard Sutcliffe from the 'Athletic' had arranged to meet me and take a picture for his up coming article. Great bloke but I will keep who he supports between the two of us. Then see and say hi to Kevin McCabe. After eventually sorting a safe spot for my bike we went to meet Paul's Mum and Niece. Paul's mum is amazing. Not seen her for years and she looks no different and still travels by coach to the away games. The ground is starting to look tired. No, not in comparison to the Lane or other older grounds but to Tottenhams new space ship. Give me BDTBL any day. The Blades start the game well.

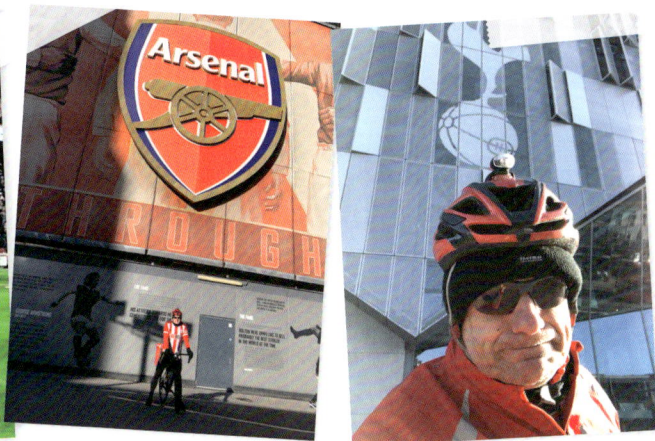

Pressing against a nervous looking Arsenal. Mid way through the first half we decide to stop passing to our players and give them more of the game. 1-0 to the Arsenal soon after. The games gone flat. We need someone to make a crunching challenge or anything to get us up for it. I include us fans in that too. Second half begins much the same. The reason I love Chris Wilder is he doesn't mess about. He had obviously given it to the players at half time but things hadn't really changed so he changed things. We had more of the ball but I just felt we lacked the cutting edge today. That's why I don't have a career in football. Fleck, on the half volley fizzes one. 1-1. GET IN. The usual declaring my love for a complete stranger with a beard commences. Good result. Yes Arsenal are no where near where they were

but we've met em half way. Run to my bike as booked stupidly the 5.30 out of St Pancras. Shit the Garmin has froze. Haven't time to bugger about with it so followed my nose. Did well to be fair and arrived with 15 minutes to spare. Make that 45 minutes delayed AGAIN. A great journey home, not, sat on floor next to bike. 12 done 7 to go. Another great contact via Twitter who'd seen Chris' video, Jess who works for the BBC got in touch. So on the Tuesday before the Palace game I'm sat with Harry Gration and Keeley Donavon in the Look North Studio. Brilliant opportunity to spread the word. It proved the case as I had about 20 donations within an hour. Leeds fans, Wednesday fans amongst them. When i think about the pathetic banter between fans I shake my head, especially when we all come together for poorly children.

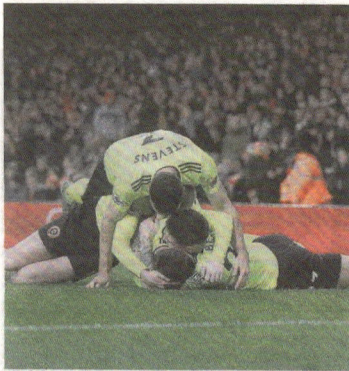

Sheffield United's John Fleck celebrates scoring his sides first goal

Blades claim a late point at the Emirates

The secret behind Fleck's success for United is revealed

JAMES SHIELD
The Star's Blades writer

Email: james.shield@jpimedia.co.uk
Twitter: @JamesShield1

ARSENAL 1
UNITED 1

The teams

Arsenal: Leno, Lacazette (Nketiah 74), Ozil, Torreira, Maitland-Niles, Pepe, Mustafi, Luiz, Xhaka, Martinelli, Saka. Not used: Martinez, Bellerin, Ceballos, Holding, Willock, Guendouzi.

Sheffield United: Henderson, Basham (Besic 77), Egan, O'Connell, Stevens, Baldock, Norwood, Fleck, Lundstram (Robinson 67), McBurnie, Mousset (Sharp 54). Not used: Verrips, Jagielka, K Freeman, Osborn.

Referee: Mike Dean (The Wirral).

Chris Wilder called it "ridiculous" after watching his side start the match well and end it strongly but sometimes labour in between.

'Significant' would have been a better description, as Sheffield United are now mastering the art of avoiding defeat whenever they fail to fire.

John Fleck's late goal, his fifth since helping Wilder's squad gain promotion last term, denied Arsenal the three points which appeared to be heading their way following Gabriel Martinelli's well-crafted opener.

A scruffy finish – the ball bouncing into the turf before spiralling into the back of the net – the midfielder's strike probably reflected United's performance. After initially troubling Mikel Arteta's star-studded side with their energy and movement, Wilder acknowledged they had sometimes ridden their luck before being rewarded for showing great resilience and persistence.

"If you can get a result without playing well," the visiting manager acknowledged afterwards, "Then that's a good quality."

Despite facing opponents with over £280m worth of talent at their disposal, it was United who created the best two openings of the game before Martinelli turned home Bukayo Saka's centre on the stroke of half-time.

Chris Wilder acknowledges the crowd at the Emirates Stadium

Lys Mousset, parting Oli McBurnie in attack, headed an Enda Stevens cross over the bar before missing the target again from even closer range soon after. Although an offside flag had been raised, video replays suggested the 'goal' would have stood had the Frenchman hit the target.

As United lost their rhythm, so Arsenal's influence grew.

The shape of his body, the way he adjusted position and traced the flight of the ball before threading it into the back of Bernd Leno's net, provided the clues.

An hour after John Fleck earned Sheffield United a draw against Arsenal, Chris Wilder delivered the confirmation.

The midfielder, he revealed, grew-up scoring rather than creating goals.

"He started out as a centre-forward," said the United manager, tracing Fleck's journey from teenage protege at Rangers to Premier League footballer. "Technically he's really good.

"That was John's position to begin with, I believe. That's why he knows what he's doing and has got the ability."

Having initially struggled, Fleck's late equaliser suggests the 28-year-old is now equipped physically, tactically and mentally to fulfil the promise which once saw him dubbed Scotland's answer to Wayne Rooney.

Fleck's strike in north London was his fifth of the campaign; more than he achieved during five seasons at Ibrox, a brief spell with Blackpool and, following four in Coventry City colours, his previous three with United.

Speaking before the trip to London, Wilder insisted the player himself must take the lion's share of the credit for his emergence as one of the top-flight's most effective midfielders.

But Fleck's rise to prominence can also be attributed to a decision taken inside Bramall Lane's bootroom way back in August when coaching staff began devising ways of ensuring United could perform effectively at the highest level.

"He's getting that belief and the system suits him," Wilder explained. "Instead of playing in a 'two', he's now got that licence to get up the pitch more and we're seeing the benefits of that.

"Sometimes, you've got to look at the players you've got and tweak things a bit.

"You can't just sit in for 90 minutes. You've got to have people who can score and open things up."

Part idealist – devising his own take on the 3-5-2 shape after taking charge four years ago – Wilder's solution to the problem of how to unlock Fleck's potential confirms he also possesses a pragmatic streak.

Mikel Arteta had clearly tasked Granit Xhaka to operate as an auxiliary defender whenever Arsenal seized possession, allowing Bukayo Saka to charge upfield and prevent his fellow wing-back George Baldock from doing likewise, which in turn limited the effectiveness of United's overlapping centre-halves.

It proved a successful ploy, with Saka delivering the cross, following an interchange between Mesut Ozil and Alexandre Lacazette, which allowed Martinelli to convert.

With even better players at their disposal, Manchester City, who travel to South Yorkshire on Tuesday, could attempt something similar.

"I wasn't surprised we were behind at the interval, because they had grown into the game," Wilder said. "But I'm pleased we took a point because we always give ourselves a chance with our attitude.

"We have to play a lot better than that, though, to pick up points over a period of time."

It is a measure of United's progress, however, that despite dominating possession, an Arsenal squad which cost nearly £300 million to assemble struggled to translate that figure into clear cut chances.

Indeed United crafted the best two chances of the game: Lys Mousset heading wide from Enda Stevens before glancing over from close-range. Adjudged offside by the assistant referee, video replays

John Fleck celebrates scoring

suggested VAR would have overturned that decision had the Frenchman hit the target.

The introduction of Billy Sharp, the first of two brave changes by United, helped them wrestle back the momentum.

Only a fine interception by Shkrodran Mustafi prevented Oliver Norwood's pass from reaching an unmarked Sharp on the edge of the six yard box, before the United captain's presence ensured a cross by his fellow substitute Callum Robinson reached Fleck for the equaliser.

"John tackles, he wins headers and he wins races," said Wilder. "He's a proper midfielder for me."

Sheffield United

John Fleck scores for United at the Emirates

Superb early cross created a great chance for Moucset but he couldn't get his header on target

Arsenal's Nicolas Pepe and Sheffield United's Enda Stevens battle for the ball

Highlight

John Fleck's late equaliser sent United's Scottish hero tumbling to the turf after an attempted knee slide went wrong. It was probably his only misstep all afternoon. Psychologically the goal was important, after back to back defeats to Manchester City and Liverpool left United's long and proud unbeaten run in tatters. For Fleck, it was a moment that capped another impressive display which saw him drive from deep with the ball with real tenacity, and no little skill either. The former Rangers prodigy has probably taken longer than many predicted to really blossom at the top level, but how United are benefitting as a result. Fleck is reaping the rewards of a change of shape, and United haven't looked back either.

Lowlight

Despite taking another point at the Emirates, there is always the thought lurking that it should have been three – both against Arsenal and other top flight opponents this season. Saturday's statistics are plain – 12 shots, but only four on target, one goal. While United have defied those who doubted they would even survive in the Premier League and showed their quality by knocking on the door of European contention, the wasting of opportunities is chipping away at their successes – they have dropped to seventh in the table.

As Chris Wilder said: "When teams don't put you to bed, we have an opportunity to get something from the game. We need to play a lot better than that for us to regularly pick up points."

Oli McBurnie takes on Ainsley Maitland-Niles

CHAPTER 13

Crystal Palace, 1st February

Really looking forward to this one as my mate Paul is riding with me and Wayne doing backup. The three of us used to go everywhere with the Blades in the bad old days. Despite the Blades being useless back then we never stopped laughing. Quotes like 'I'm never coming again' to be shortly followed by 'what time we setting off next week?'

Having suffered with man flu now for the whole of December and January I was hoping to clear the remaining snot on this ride.
I recently had to change my cleats although I wasn't convinced it was the cleats but the bike shop were adamant. I wish I'd checked them out! Set off and the right shoe wouldn't fix into the pedal. Cycled on one leg to the shop and got new pedals, great start. The weather was tropical! Well slight exaggeration there, what I mean is it wasn't raining. Still there was my old friend the head wind. Great riding with Paul, nice to chat instead of going into my usual cycle zone out mode.

It wasn't long until Paul joined my world as he said, as we approached another climb, 'guess were going up that fucker?' Had to giggle.
Wayne was his usual dry as a desert self. At the meeting points he mentioned how tiring getting in and out the car is. Made the first nights stop in a decent time, well at least it was still light. Dinner with Wayne and Paul sharing memories and new stories. Paul needs to go public on when he and a mate booked tickets for Ritchie Blackmore's Rainbow, or was the Geoffreys Rainbow, FFS so funny but just wished they'd chosen to collect on the door.
Strange to think that this will be the last time I stop at The Royal Oak at

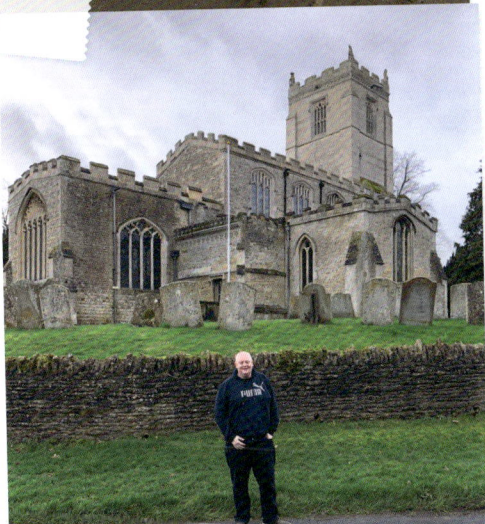

Duddington, on this adventure anyway.
Said my farewells to the
Landlord and off we go.
First 30 miles were very pleasant apart
from an increasingly strong wind. I'm
really enjoying this ride, combination
of having Wayne and Paul with me
and the weather being better.
Stopped at the Courtyard Coffee shop
again for my catch up with the Locals.
This place has a great feel about it.
Wished them all well and
went on our way.
The wind was really strong now
and with rain in the air our
pace slowed right down.
Paul is doing really well
in these conditions.
Wayne keeping us updated on the
transfer deadline latest. Never known
so much happening for the Blades
as we break our record again!
3 years ago seems such a distant memory.
Eventually make it to The Feathers.
One of those nights that can't be
planned. The three of us ripping
the shit out of everyone.
Paul gets the beers in, but curiosity
gets the better of him when asking
why the guest beer is called 'beer'
The answer was they hadn't

a name for it, so Paul got a pen and christened it 'Blade on a Bike'

Some guy (in our opinion) decides to hire an escort and requests she dresses as Cat woman. At first we take the piss out of ourselves for making this up BUT it potentially is true. The guy is all over the place trying to order drinks. Not pissed but must be stoned? We ain't a clue cos we're old gits who ain't done no shit. A tough day ends AGAIN with us laughing. Saturday morning and the yellow ball in the sky decides to join us. Maybe 5 too many Peronis and that double Glenfiddich give a fuzzy feel to the start of another very windy ride. Need to keep an eye on the pace and time as a bit further than normal on match day. Really enjoy the route through London and over London Bridge but shit there's a lot of traffic lights. Get to White Hart Lane, AGAIN in no time and before long we're on London Bridge asking the Russians to take our photo. Then from across the road theres a 'go on Blades' then I look round and there's a man mountain in my face 'are you charity bloke?' He smiles, and hands me £20. Unreal. Stop at lights at Elephant and Castle to a chorus of 'we are Blades, we are Blades' Having to part with my touring bike after the Liverpool trip was hard to take but the sudden realisation that I may have to turn the life support machine off for my 'focus' (roadbike) is heartbreaking. Lots of clunks and groans

from a friend I've had 7 years now.
Served me well and probably has more
miles on the clock than most cars.
I decided against telling Paul that we
finish with a steep climb but when
he sees the transmitter above us he
knows what's coming. Nice last mile
downhill and we're there. Paul has been
brilliant company and done brilliantly.
Wayne pulled a reight parking space
out his magic hat. We change in the
street and head for the ground.
In the ground all I want is a tea,
Jesus how Rock n Roll am I.
Interesting to see our new Norwegian
hero makes the starting 11. Not
something CW normally does so he

must be something special. A dull
first half passes us by. Trying to
get to the bog at halftime was
like stepping back in time 30 years.
Very cozy, let's leave it at that.
The Blades start taking control in
the 2nd half. I'm gonna call out Billy
Sharp now. This guy is one of us and
living our dream. He had the chance
of playing football every week at a
top Championship team but chose to
stay with us. He's worked his bollocks
off today and was only fitting that
his never say die attitude won us the
corner that won us the game. Thoroughly
nice bloke as well. Cheers Billy.
The 3 of us old gits hugged and

nearly danced about at the final whistle.
I needed help getting down off the seat
I'd decided to stand on. Took forever
to get home but my what another great
day to be a Blade. 5th ffs. We are now
better odds to finish 4th than Arsenal.
When the guy on the radio announced
that the 3 of us burst out laughing.
Cuddling Lola late Saturday I look at the
Justgiving page and to my astonishment
my £5000 target has been smashed. The
uncontrollable emotion brought floods of
tears to a very happy man. Decision made
I'm upping the target to 10k and now
committing to cycle to the cup games as well.
This weird half baked winter break saw
us playing Bournemouth at home at 2pm
on Sunday whilst most other teams were
in Dubai. O wait we're off next week.
Surprised they didn't put this match on
box office asking for £30 subscriptions.
Can't believe the game went ahead due to
storm Ciara. Why on earth they have to
name the storms I don't know. And have you
noticed how excited the weather forecasters
get when there's an 'Amber' weather
warning. So when's there a green warning?
Prior to this match I liked Bournemouth
and how they had maintained their Premier
League status on such limited resources.
Post match I really hope relegation hits them

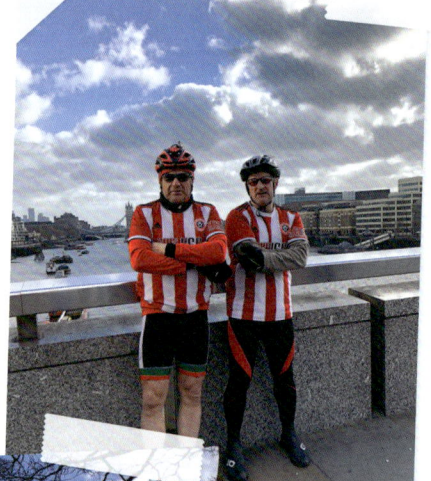

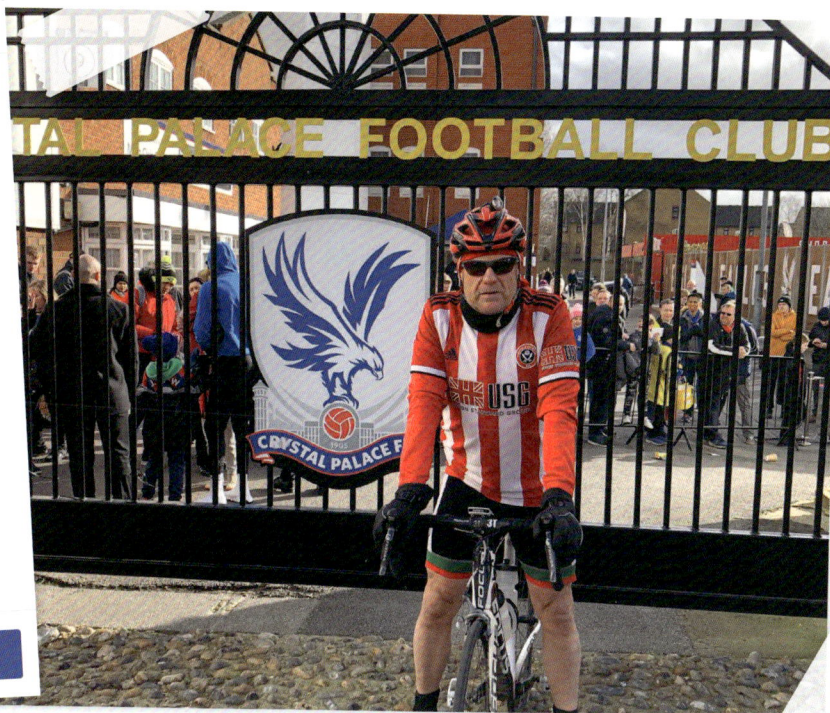

hard and their cry baby players beg Chris Wilder for a chance. Well I can tell em now they have Bob and no Hope. Pathetic diving and feigning injury trying to get our players booked. Gosling post match even had the cheek to call out the ref for taking the piss out of them. So fifth place and getting very twitchy at my stupid statement of cycling to Champions League group stage matches. Friday 14th...Lola and I having a romantic evening in when the news lands that Man City have been banned from Europe. O FFS seriously getting worried cos might have mentioned cycling to Champions League group stage matches. Another sell out for the

visit of Brighton.
I've been climbing the walls for the past two weeks since the Palace trip. The weather has been shite for what feels like an eternity. So decide to cycle to the Lane for this one. Bad mistake! Even though I'm a fat swine I was still getting blown all over the shop. Really dangerous and shitting self if honest. Get there and tie bike up to cycle hoops behind kop. Great performance against Brighton including a wonder strike from Edna! (My Nan was called Edna, that's why). All disappointed with draw but god what a season this is.

New boys can raise Blades standards even more: boss

James Shield
james.shield@jpimedia.co.uk
@jameshield1

Blades boss Chris Wilder has identified the influence he expects players like Sander Berge, Panos Retsos and Richairo Zivkovic to exert after arriving at Bramall Lane.

It stretches, he insisted, across the entire first team squad.

Because their presence, if last January's recruitment drive is anything to go by, will coax even greater levels of performance out of United's longer serving players.

"They'll improve the current crop," Wilder said.

"People coming in always does that.

"It's in the psyche of a footballer, when they see someone new turning up, to think 'I want to show you how good I am, and if you're coming for me, then I'm going to put in even more.'

"It will raise the standards of everyone which should impact on results."

Wilder pointed to the effect of United's manoeuvres in the market this time last term to support his theory.

Fourth in the Championship table after beating Blackburn Rovers 3-0 at Bramall Lane on December 29,

they went on to secure automatic promotion after capturing Gary Madine, Scott Hogan and Kieran Dowell on loan.

Although all three left at the end of the campaign, Wilder said: "You saw with those, how it lifted the whole group.

"Bringing them in, and they all contributed, was a huge part of how things turned out."

United were languishing in League One when Wilder was appointed in the summer of 2016.

But they entered Saturday's match at Crystal Palace ranked eighth in the Premier League table and, although the 52-year-old will not admit it publicly, believing they have an outside chance of qualifying for the Europa League.

Events at Selhurst Park, where United triumphed 1-0, served to further strengthen United's credentials.

"It was a really good window for us," Wilder said, after United paid £22m to sign Berge.

"Everyone says it's difficult but it's been successful recently.

"The first in League One was big for us and the one back in the Championship was difficult.

"But last season, that was a big one."

Sheffield United's manager Chris Wilder celebrates after the Premier League match at Selhurst Park, London: Paul Terry/Sportimage

Baldock may have seen red for fouls on Zaha: Roy

Roy Hodgson claimed George Baldock could have been sent-off for fouling Wilfried Zaha "time after time" during Sheffield United's win over Crystal Palace.

Baldock spent much of the first-half walking a disciplinary tightrope after being cautioned for a foul on Zaha early in the match.

Referee Andy Madley stopped play again 10 minutes before the interval following another challenge between the pair but ignored the home players' pleas to dismiss the United wing-back.

Hodgson, who later saw one of his own defenders - Joel Ward - shown a red card before it was downgraded to a yellow, said: "I saw Wilf fouled time after time, which eventually led to a yellow card, and then I saw him fouled again so it could have been a red."

Crystal Palace's manager Roy Hodgson

Trio face steep learning curve in crash course playing Blades way

Sheffield United's latest signings will continue their crash course in the tactics and strategies Chris Wilder's squad employ ahead of Sunday's game against AFC Bournemouth.

Richairo Zivkovic, Panos Retsos and Sander Berge, who became the most expensive player in United's history after completing his £22m move from Genk last week, enjoyed a brief introduction to the demands of Wilder's preferred 3-5-2 system before the 1-0 win over Crystal Palace.

Although Wilder is of the belief that intelligent players master new challenges quicker than others, he confirmed United's match analysts have been preparing a series of dossiers to help accelerate the process.

"They're all experienced boys," Wilder, who also unveiled Jack Robinson and Jack Rodwell earlier in the window, said. "They'll be doing all the video analysis stuff, showing what happens because they've been brought in for specific positions. They'll get all the information they need.

"But we wouldn't have signed them if we didn't think they could do a job for us."

Berge made his full debut at Selhurst Park, being replaced by John Lundstram midway through the second-half.

Confirming no one is guaranteed a place in his starting eleven, Wilder explained why it is important the new arrivals grasp their roles quickly.

"They could go in straight away," he said. "There's injuries, suspensions to consider. And loss of form. But when they're in, they've got to stay in. We're not buying players as projects."

Top Tweets

Speaking after the game, Wilder was full of praise for debutant Sander Berge: "He looks like a Sheffield United player – he's big, he's strong and he's athletic. He's a good footballer."

And on Twitter, United fans were equally impressed with Berge and their team's showing.

@JeniParker4: "Overlapping centre halves with nine clean sheets and fifth in the Premier League who would have thought it?"

@keithwall1955 #twitterblades: "I have been supporting the Blades for over 50 years and I have to say this is the best it has ever been and I believe it will get better. Wilder is by far the best manager that either club in Sheffield has ever had."

@daveag: "I mean, seriously. What player wouldn't just love to play for @SheffieldUnited. Kid's first game and they sing to him as if he's already a legend."

@DuncanPayne1: "I keep expecting to wake up from a long and happy dream. Then I realise this is real. Sheffield United are fifth in the PL with two thirds of the season gone. And then I really start to dream."

@RobPNicholso: "Ugly win that. But good teams win ugly. Twelve points clear of relegation zone!"

@ThomasCarter83: "Berge looked tidy enough today. It won't take him long to fully bed in in that midfield, a very intelligent footballer with real quality on the ball. #twitterblades."

@jarnij10: "Chris Wilder brought everybody together at every level in the club, love the man #GOAT #sufc #twitterblades."

Sheffield United

Jack O'Connell celebrates as Palace keeper Vicente Guaita fumbles.

Berge's debut shows it's money well spent as Blades handed win

JAMES SHIELD
The Star's Blades writer
Email: james.shield@jpimedia.co.uk
Twitter: @JamesShield1

Chris Wilder makes his point

United showing no signs of dropping off

PALACE	0
BLADES	1

It seemed strange, almost perverse even, that after showcasing their tactical discipline, Sheffield United prevailed thanks to calamitous goalkeeping mistake.

But then again, even though Crystal Palace manager Roy Hodgson later insisted Vicente Guaita had been undone by the weather rather than the visitors' powers of concentration, perhaps not.

As a swirling wind swept across the pitch inside Selhurst Park, United's rigid adherence to the game plan Chris Wilder had devised helped ensure this match was still balanced on a knife edge when the Spaniard, miscalculating the flight of Oliver Norwood's corner, gathered the ball and then dropped it back across his line.

By Wilder's own admission, United "didn't produce" their "most free flowing performance" of the season against opponents who, for long periods of the first-half, threatened through Jordan Ayew and Wilfried Zaha.

However, with new record signing Sander Berge making his debut in midfield, they demonstrated a pragmatism which, with the race for a top six finish so delicately poised, should serve them well over the coming months.

Guaita's error came early

The teams

Crystal Palace: Guaita, Ward, van Aanholt, Milivojevic, Tomkins, Ayew, Zaha, Benteke (Townsend 74), McArthur (Kouyate 85), McCarthy (Meyer 79), Cahill. Not used: Hennessey, Dann, Kouyate, Kelly, Riedewald. **Sheffield United:** Henderson, Baldock, Stevens, O'Connell, Egan, Basham, Norwood, Fleck, Berge (Lundstram 67), Sharp (Mousset 62), McBurnie (Osborn 90). Not used: Verrips, L Freeman, Jagielka, Robinson. **Referee:** Andrew Madley

Sander Berge challenges Patrick van Aanholt

in the second period when Norwood swept a set-piece across the area and, having elected not to punch clear, the 33-year-old seemed to panic after losing his balance.

It proved to be the defining moment of a contest where chances, until the action inevitably became stretched during the closing stages, were at a premium.

A picture doing the rounds before kick-off showed Chris Wilder, then in charge of Oxford, cheering on the team he now manages from the stands at Selhurst Park.

Eleven years after it was taken, Sheffield United's latest trip to Crystal Palace spawned another iconic image; Sander Berge, beaded in sweat and arms outstretched, paying homage to his new club's supporters following a hugely significant win in the capital.

Less than two hours earlier Berge, a 21-year-old Norway international, had made his full Blades debut following his £22 million move from Genk.

The most expensive player in United's history, Wilder later joked he owed his starting role to the size of his price tag before explaining, with an icy stare to hammer home the point, that actually it was because of the youngster's tactical acumen.

"The owner told me I had to play him," Wilder replied when asked why Berge had been parachuted straight into the the starting eleven, despite only being unveiled on Thursday.

"He was adamant that we weren't paying that kind of money just to put someone on the bench.

"No, seriously, we'd tracked him for a while, he'd trained with us and we thought it would give us a boost."

Predictably, despite being regarded as one of the most promising midfielders in Europe, Berge suffered a couple of early missteps before beginning to find his feet.

A run into the penalty area, during the opening skirmishes

of a contest settled by Vicente Guaita's goalkeeping howler, was timed a little too late to connect with John Fleck's centre.

It was quickly followed, as they fathomed each other's positional preferences, by a clunky exchange of passes with Oliver Norwood.

But it was after that mistake, which threatened to send Palace's Patrick van Aanholt surging into United's half, when Berge began to demonstrate why he should prove such an invaluable addition to Wilder's squad.

Already known as an accomplished technician, he darted back and regained possession rather than expecting someone else to clear up the mess. Tellingly, it was also the last obvious error that Berge made.

"That's the reason we chucked him in," Wilder continued. "Because we know he's an intelligent player.

"We took him on board for 48 hours, talked to him and set up some fundamental aspects that he needed to know about how we go about things.

"But I thought Palace did as good a job as anyone on us in the first-half. They really jumped on us."

As Wilder acknowledged, Roy Hodgson's side caused United plenty of problems before Guaita's own goal – he spilled Norwood's second-half corner across the line – decided the outcome of the game.

Wilder's pioneering system, which revolves around attacking centre-halves and marauding wing-backs, can be difficult for opponents to make

sense of. But Hodgson, one of England's most experienced coaches, had clearly done his homework.

The same can also be said of Berge who, after being thrown in at the deep end, quickly adapted to its demands and challenges. A towering presence, his poise and touch also made a positive impression.

After the final whistle the travelling Blades fans made their feelings known, serenading Berge to the tune of Oasis' 'She's Electric'.

John Lundstram, who replaced Berge during the closing stages, also impressed after being introduced.

His performance, coupled with the one produced by

fellow substitute Lys Mousset, provided Wilder with exactly the type of headache he wants ahead of Sunday's game against AFC Bournemouth. The Blades are now ranked sixth in the Premier League.

"I thought the performance of John and Mousset when they came on was just typical of their attitudes," Wilder said. "Lunny has been out for a couple of games but he came roaring back.

"Bash [Chris Basham] got beaten up, he's got a massive cut on his knee and a knock to his head which will possibly need a couple of stitches.

"But the boys, every single one of them, really dug in," he added.

CHAPTER 14

Reading, 3rd March

Having decided to do the cup games now after surpassing my initial £5,000 target an early set off on a beautiful sunny but cold Monday was just what I needed.

The weather has been horrendous and the Coronavirus is spreading like wild fire throughout the world. All the experts keep telling us to keep our hands clean with soap and water. Surely if that kills the virus wouldn't drinking soap and water do the same? Alex, my cycle buddy is riding down to Reading with me but has no interest in football whatsoever. Felt unfit today, had a shite week last week so had too many beers and shit food Great to be doing a different route from London. Today is the same route as Bournemouth day 1, Christ that seems ages ago. Interesting to see all the rivers take over the

surrounding fields. Had a rather dodgy moment in the afternoon while cycling on a section of closed road. Alex didn't see (god knows how) the large section of road that had no tarmac on it so a good foot drop, and nearly had me in it. So good not having a strong headwind but did start feeling it as we got past 80 miles. Arrive at Tarsus Hotel in Southam before 4.30pm which was some achievement. Lovely food as usual.

The weather chap said tomorrow (Tuesday) would be sunny and 10 degrees.

So when I woke to rain I was really pissed off. The first 25 miles saw me really mardy. We stopped at a really posh place at Holt just after Deddington. For some reason I was starving and ate several egg mayo sandwiches. It was bloody freezing and I pushed my legs hard to get warmer. Started feeling stronger and in no time we stopped again at a nice café with 15 miles to go. It was most down hill from there with a 20 degree decent into Whitchurch on Thames. Beautiful place. The route then took us along a river through woods. The bike needs a really keen clean now. Made it at about 4.30pm and had the usual photo. Not many folk about. Just as I was explaining to Alex that I normally get home fans saying 'you ain't cycled it have you?' a guy walked up asking just that. After a rather tiring conversation the guy asked 'have you got £7' tha what, I asked. That's the north south divide for you, bloody beggars in Sheffield only ask for 50p. Surprised he didn't say I take card... Met Paul at the Hotel and the 3 of us had a quick meal

then off to cheer the Wizards on.
Good start with Dids at last
getting on the scoresheet.
We seemed to start well and then got
worse as the game went on. They were
awarded the softest penalty ever. Baldy
touched their guy and that was it, he went
down holding his leg, work that one out.
Mixed feelings as the game went on. Seen that
Newcastle had won at WBA so it's possible
I could be cycling to the north east 2 weeks
running. When Billy came on and scored the
winner that possibility came a touch closer.
The short 4 mile ride to Reading station the
following morning was pleasant enough. Said my
farewells to Alex who, believe it or not is cycling
all the way home in one go. An Audax they call
it (300KM) i would call it something else.
Watching our South Barnsley neighbours
the following day prior to the cup draw
made me realise how far we had progressed
and how far they had gone backwards. I
nearly felt sorry for them but couldn't if I'm
honest. My Mums words ringing in my ears 'no
James, my Father was a Wednesday fan.'
Willing a home draw, I was delighted
when Number 2, Sheffield United, came
out first. Home to Arsenal, so perhaps
two more trips to London, who knows.
Home to Norwich, let's not be complacent Blades.
Cycle down again, it's actually quicker as, although

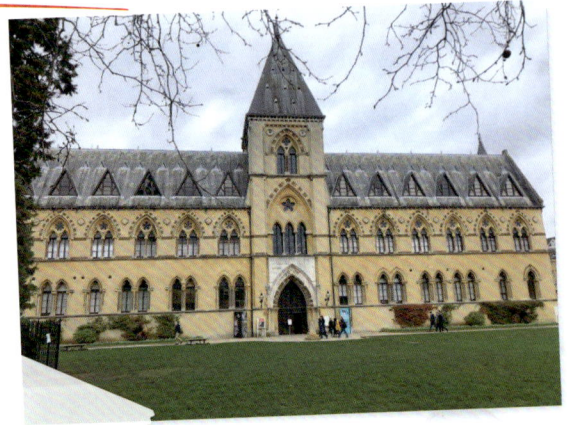

Oxford, lovely place!

8 miles, by the time you park top side of Heeley I am locking my bike behind the Kop. Real strange I thought, seeing football fans actually washing their hands after having a piss. This Virus thing is getting worrying. It's been mentioned that if it gets much worse they will have to play behind closed doors. FFS that would be a nightmare. The Blades do the business and that man Billy Sharp whose seen our transfer record broken 3 times this season is there to head home the winner.

Today felt a huge watershed moment in my mind for Sheffield football. We look good for at least a top half finish in the Premier League and our (not so massive) neighbours have just been hammered 5-0 by Brentford. Great times to be a Blade.

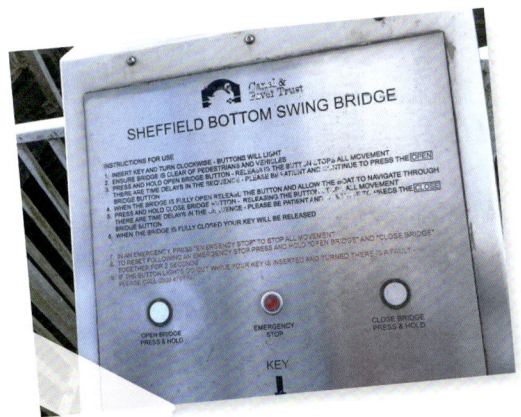

United set their sights on making history in the FA Cup

James Shield
james.shield@jpimedia.co.uk
@JamesShield1

Sheffield United have been in the business of making history, not reliving it, since Chris Wilder became manager.

But when they return to Bramall Lane from Reading, the 52-year-old and his players might take a moment to reflect on the 95 years that have passed since the FA Cup was last in the club's possession.

But the Blades are now tantalisingly close to regaining it after goals from David McGoldrick and Billy Sharp saw them reach the last eight. George Puscas had earlier equalised when Reading were awarded a soft penalty.

"I don't know where the players can take this season," Wilder said, again praising the "attitude" of his group.

"Because what they just do is roll on to the next challenge. The way they take on board what is put in front of them, and just get on with the job, is something else. It's a brilliant position to be in."

Speaking before United's success in the third round, over non-league AFC Fylde, Wilder had sounded incredulous when the idea was put to him that his squad might reach May's showpiece.

"I think that's a little too far away in terms of our development. We've got it all on establishing ourselves in this division, let alone start thinking about something else."

He adopted the same approach less than one month, after being drawn with Millwall. But following that victory at The Den, something changed. Wilde began to suspect, albeit privately, that what he had previously thought impossible might be possible after all.

"You just want to progress and see where it takes you," he said after United's latest success. "That's all we look at; the very next game. We knew this wouldn't be easy because our own club has had a habit of knocking out Premier League sides in the past and Reading, who I thought were inspired by their crowd by the way, have some really talented lads."

Ben Osborn, starting last night's match in place of Enda Stevens who is still nursing a calf problem, had described United's performance in south-east London as the template they should follow.

"We were clinical," he reflected. "We were ruthless. We took our chances and limited them to very few."

Osborn, despite being among the more junior members of United's dressing room, led by example when he started the move which led to McGoldrick's second minute opener.

Seizing possession in midfield with a crunching tackle which sent Luke Freeman scampering forward, he then demanded the ball back and produced a perfectly flighted cross which the striker, scoring for the first time in 23 outings for United, could not fail to head home.

Wilder, who believes McGoldrick's worth should be measured in more than simply goals, will nevertheless have been delighted the Republic of Ireland has now got that monkey off his back.

The player himself appeared mighty relieved too; going about his business with a freedom and a purpose which magnified his polished technique and skills.

With John Lundstram operating further forward after being recalled to the starting eleven, Sander Berge found himself back on familiar territory just in front of the back four.

It was probably no surprise, therefore, that he produced arguably his best showing in United colours after leaving Belgium. Berge and Lundstram, for all the right reasons, have provided Wilder with plenty of food for thought ahead of Saturday's home game against Norwich City.

George Baldock did the same two minutes before half-time, although the United defender could count himself desperately unlucky to concede the spot-kick which drew Reading level.

Yes, he placed his hands on Andy Rinomhota's back. Yes, there was contact. But nowhere near enough to send the youngster tumbling over. Puscas, who despite his name is Romanian, ensured the hosts were able to exploit referee Kevin Friend's generosity when he netted for the 13th time this term.

"What really pleased me," Wilder said. "Was that we found a way to get the result.

"We've had senior staff at both of Reading's last two games but we knew this would be a different Reading side we were up against."

"Gary Rowett at Millwall praised the consistency of our attitude," Wilder added. "And Mark [Bowen, the Reading manager] did it before we came here. So that's good to hear."

It was a measure of both Reading's tenacity and United's determination that Wilder introduced Oli McBurnie and Sharp during the closing stages. Had his team been cruising, then Richairo Zivkovic would surely have been awarded a debut, like Panos Retsos..

Instead, Wilder preferred to place his faith in the hands of those already familiar with the intricacies of United's system.

However, falling short of their first half standards, the visitors were unable to avert extra-time. But Sharp scores goals. And he scored the decisive one, for the umpteenth time in his remarkable career, to send United through.

"Billy's still got life in him yet," Wilder said. "He's just a natural finisher."

David McGoldrick scores the opening goal against Reading. Picture: Michael Steele/Getty Images

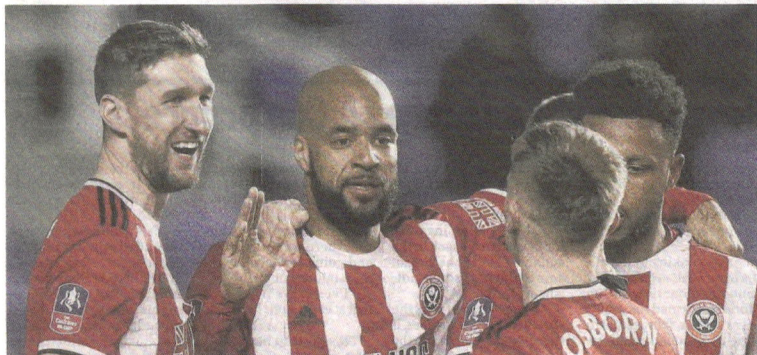
David McGoldrick celebrates scoring his first goal in 23 games

Billy Sharp wheels away after netting the winner. Picture: Sportimage

Striker McGoldrick breaks his duck at last

There have been times this season when David McGoldrick must have wondered exactly what he had to do to score.

The Sheffield United centre-forward has produced some scintillating performances, seduced his manager with the intelligence of his play and, before injury struck two months ago, regularly bemused Premier League defences.

McGoldrick's only problem was, whenever a chance presented itself, he always failed to convert.

Until this FA Cup tie at Reading that was, when his early goal laid the foundations for a win which saw Chris Wilder's side reach the quarter-finals thanks to Billy Sharp's header in extra-time.

George Puscas, once of Internazionale, had earlier drawn the hosts level with a 43rd minute penalty.

Only two minutes had passed when McGoldrick claimed his first United goal since April, when a memorable brace against Hull City effectively sealed promotion from the Championship.

Mark Bowen's men made the visitors work – with Dean Henderson punching clear from Yakou Meite – but there was no suggestion an equaliser was coming before Puscas restored parity from the spot.

The Romanian striker produced a clinical finish from 12 yards out.

United had been comfortable, perhaps even a shade too comfortable, before Puscas intervened, although it would be a mistake to suggest complacency had crept into their ranks.

As the final whistle beckoned, so Reading's belief grew. But Sharp nipped it in the bud when he pounced towards the end of the first period of extra time.

David McGoldrick celebrates scoring the first goal

CHAPTER 15

Newcastle United, 14th March

Bloody hell things are really kicking off re the Coronavirus. Lots of conflicting information. Assistant chief medical officer to the Government says that outdoor events don't pose a risk. So why now are they talking about playing games behind closed doors? In my view we're a fucking island so surely we can contain the fucker. Everyone stay in for 2 weeks FFS.

Anyway set off with less enthusiasm than normal as don't really know if we will get to see the match. Lovely sunny day albeit very windy, AGAIN!, although it was over my left shoulder. In places it was really strong blowing me into the road, don't tell mi Mum. First 40 miles really not nice as through towns that need an injection of cash. It was great to have Ashley do back up and was good to see him after 20 miles. I know I've mentioned this before but I'm really pissed off at how much litter is thrown from cars. On one road in the countryside which must have been 5 miles long there was a constant line

Received the news that
all football is postponed

of litter. Scum, the only word I have.
When my kids were young I used to play
a game when driving through villages. I'd
pip the horn and wave when going past
people, especially old uns. Most would
wave back. A point for the elderly, 2
for middle aged and 3 for youngsters.
Played it again today but on a bike.
Got a few waves. They'll be at home
now still trying to work out who I am.
Made it to Boroughbridge in good
time although the last 8 miles were
as dangerous as I've encountered
to date. The strong cross wind
kept pushing me into the road.
Nice afternoon in the pool and
evening with Ashley almost took the
mind off the impending disaster.
Wake up at 2am because some twat
has television on in next room. Ear
plugs in and back to weird dreams.
Waking up to the news that Arteta has
Coronavirus. There's absolutely no way

this match is going to happen now.
I say to Ashley to keep parking
up a couple of miles ahead as the
Premier League are meeting this
morning to discuss suspending the
season. What a weird ride.
We stop at Northallerton for
a cuppa knowing anytime we
would be heading home.
As expected the news came through.
Weird weird feeling. Bit numb on the
journey home not really knowing if/
when the season will start again.
Really need to stay positive.

COVID
DISRUPTION!

Two months have passed and so have
far too many people. To date 34,000,
madness. I guess it maybe a while till
we all get back to what we knew as

normal, if we ever do. The things we all took for granted, hugging loved ones, going for a pint and seeing them red and white wizards. My routine of walking Lola, painting the fence, doing CrossFit, walking Lola has kept my spirits at a reasonable level and I realise I'm lucky that I have wonderful countryside around me. Last week saw Boris ease restrictions slightly, meaning it's ok to travel further afield if we self distance.

Had purchased a Tacx turbo trainer, thinking I could finish the rides on that, but that was faulty from the off. Funny thing about that, Garmin (now own Tacx) wanted me to send the faulty unit back to them at Southampton at my cost. It didn't sway them a) when I said it was faulty from new and b) it weighs over 30kg and was going to cost hundreds of pounds.... what the hell has happened to customer service. So I need to get this one done (Newcastle). Anna and Jordan are moving in with me soon anyway so Social distancing will be kind of hard so decided let's get to Northallerton again and just do it. Lola will come also and see what the hell Daddy has been doing. Wide awake at 4.30am.

Arrive in Northallerton at just after 8am. I'm covered in Lola hairs. Get ready and have photo right outside Costa where 2 months previous I sat with Ashley, receiving the news that all football had been cancelled. Nothing changed there I'm afraid apart from the Bundesliga in Germany.

For some reason I feel very edgy. Not sure why. Doesn't take long to find my rhythm. In fact I purposely slow down a bit as I'm moving to fast and not really sure how my long distance fitness is. There's been a lot published about how clean the air is due to everyone being housebound for 8 weeks. I could really feel it as well. The air was so fresh and of course it wouldn't be an away trip on my bike without some rain thrown in for good measure. After the first planned meet Anna and Jordan struggled to locate me so we only met once more, in Chester-le-Street. Plenty of people about in the park. Wasn't long at all until I passed the Angel of the North.

Then across the Tyne and through the centre of Newcastle. Hardly anyone about. Such a contrast to what would have been. I climb the final mile to the towering St James Park. Get my shirt on for a quick picture then off again. Well didn't want people thinking I was a Sunderland fan. Really felt weird, very weird. On the day we should have all been celebrating the best season in my lifetime down at Southampton I was outside a deserted St James Park. No clearer knowing when football will be played again.
5 to go. Decision on when I complete will depend on where the games will be played. If they're played.

'Sorry' Blades performance leaves Wilder scratching head

James Shield
james.shield@jpimedia.co.uk
@JamesShield1

Perched on top of a hill near the famous Leazes Terrace and the site of an ancient gallows, St James' Park looms large over a city whose very sense of being is shaped by football.

It is a symbol. A cathedral. A famous place of worship where, before the Covid-19 pandemic made its way to these shores, around 40,000 devotees regularly filed through the turnstiles to watch Newcastle's players represent not only their club but also the region as a whole.

Managed and captained by lifelong supporters, Sheffield United are doing something similar in South Yorkshire.

The county might be home to five different sporting tribes. But after twice being promoted since appointing Chris Wilder, United have also become standard bearers for an area used to being let down by politicians and so puts its faith in the beautiful game instead.

Given the strength of the relationship between these teams and their people, it seemed almost cruel that this fixture was taking place behind doors.

And make no mistake, despite its significance, the funereal atmosphere inside the ground had a tangible effect on the performance of both sides.

Both United and Newcastle did their best to rouse themselves, with Wilder and Steve Bruce constantly barking instructions from the touchline. But neither team, and United in particular, were ever quite able to summon their usual verve, vigour and zip.

The difference here was not only John Egan's dismissal which, given Jack O'Connell's continuing absence leaves Wilder nursing a huge headache ahead of Wednesday's trip to Manchester United, but also the fact Newcastle were more ruthless, more clinical and approached their work with greater attention to detail.

Wilder felt all three goals United conceded were preventable. He also, alluding to the inspirational power of the visitors' fans, challenged some of those at his disposal to "give themselves a shake."

"I thought we looked a little bit sorry for ourselves and that's what really disappointed me," Wilder said.

""I haven't seen that for a long time and I didn't like it.

"Some of the lads need to give themselves a shake.

"We have to be at our maximum to get a result in this division, we can't play at 75 per cent. We have to go full tilt and we are off the pace at little bit at the moment.

"I can't quite put my finger on it because, physically, the numbers all stack up."

United arrived in the North-East ranked seventh in the table and knowing that a win would lift them to fifth. But they had also made the journey nursing a genuine grievance, after a technological malfunction had forced them to settle for a draw at Aston Villa four days earlier.

Oliver Norwood, whose free-kick had been carried into the back of the net by Orjan Nyland only for the Hawkeye system to fail, looked to take out his frustration by pinging a series of dangerous set-pieces towards Martin Dubravka.

But it was Newcastle who fashioned the best opportunity of the opening half when Miguel Almiron released Joelinton.

Even from the top of the Jackie Milburn stand, Wilder's sigh of relief was audible when the Brazilian shot tamely.

With John Fleck returning to the starting eleven after recovering from the injury which forced him to miss the trip to the West Midlands, United had earlier created some chances of their own.

Jack Robinson was inches away from meeting Norwood's centre towards the far post before another cross from the midfielder forced Martin Dubravka to scramble clear.

But disaster struck soon after the interval when Egan, who had already been cautioned following a minor confrontation with Joelinton, was dismissed for hauling back the former Hoffenheim centre-forward.

Perhaps, on the evidence of the first-half, the Republic of Ireland defender would have been better advised to simply let Joelinton dart through – even though he later netted for the first time in the competition since August.

"The first yellow was for nothing," Wilder said. "John tries to take a kick quickly, their lad stops the ball, and then they stand up to each other.

"I had no problem with what either of them did and, I've got to say, both Steve Bruce and I were stunned their both got booked for that."

"Mentally, it's strange," Bruce, Wilder's opposite number, admitted when asked about the challenge of competing in front of four empty stands.

"It feels like a reserve game, and we've all been to those, so you've got to work so hard to get your usual intensity."

Egan had only just reached the dressing room when Newcastle took the lead.

Matt Ritchie's pass into the area should have been cut out by Enda Stevens but the wing-back, usually one of the more dependable players, made a hash of his attempted clearance, allowing Allan Saint-Maximin to score.

"The goals we've conceded have been poor ones," Wilder said.

"For three goals to go in the way they did, Newcastle didn't really have to work that hard for them. And it shouldn't have been like that."

Despite finding themselves at a numerical disadvantage, United should have drawn level soon afterwards when Billy Sharp escaped his marker in front of goal. But, after stooping to meet George Baldock's cross, he directed his header wide.

Ritchie ensured that error was punished in the most devastating manner possible when he powered home from distance past Dean Henderson.

It was a superb finish but the Scot was afforded too much time and space before, as United's rearguard fathomed how to deal with the situation, being allowed to pick his spot.

Newcastle's third – Almiron squaring for Joelinton after getting in behind – was simplicity itself.

Billy Sharp looks dejected at St James' Park. Photo: Laurence Griffiths/Getty

John Egan fouls Joelinton resulting in a second yellow. Photo: AFP/Getty

Manager's fury at ref over Egan's red card

Sheffield United manager Chris Wilder criticised referee David Coote's decision to show John Egan a red card during his team's defeat at Newcastle, insisting the centre-half's dismissal had changed the dynamic of the game.

Although Wilder had no complaints about the second caution Egan received – hauling back Joelinton as the centre-forward powered towards the box – he felt the Republic of Ireland international was harshly treated after being book for a minor confrontation with the Brazilian during the opening period of the contest.

Insisting his opposite number Steve Bruce had also been surprised by how Coote chose to deal with the first tangle between the pair, Wilder said: "John tried to take a quick free-kick and their lad tried to stop it. I've got no problems with that, because it's part and parcel of the game.

"The ref pushes them away and both Steve and I were stunned that they got yellows for that. I think Steve will have been delighted in a sense though because he'll have known, being in the position he's in, that John will have been putting himself about much more than Joelinton.

"The game hasn't changed that much and, if it has, then it's in a worse place that it was before."

Egan received his marching orders for another tangle with Joelinton soon after the restart.

Newcastle took the lead soon afterwards, when the excellent Allan Saint-Maximin capitalised on a mistake by Enda Stevens before Matt Ritchie doubled the hosts' advantage.

Oliver Norwood looks dejected after the final whistle. Photo: Michael Regan/PA Wire/Pool

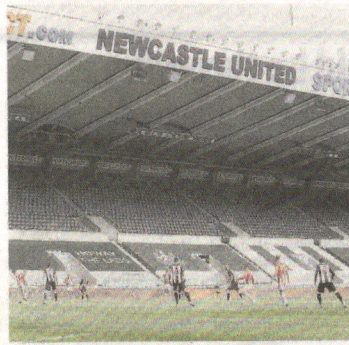

The lack of atmosphere at St James Park hit both teams

Chris Wilder speaks with the officials at full-time

5th June

So we have fixtures. Villa away on the 17th June, 6pm KO.

Will plan to set off at 6am so I can get back in time to watch it.

We are living in crazy times at the moment. This has to end before people start losing the plot.

CHAPTER 16

Aston Villa, 17th June

Wow, I guess under normal circumstances we would be well into preseason matches now, instead we restart. Like most people emotions have been running high. Black Lives Matter has for the past couple of weeks forced COVID from the main headlines. Dreadful event replacing a dreadful event.

Have to be honest and say I've really been struggling these past couple of weeks. I've always been kind of a loner but struggled with it recently. Evening before the trip to Villa. I'm sat watching the hose dampen the grass. Don't know why I'm bothering cos we all know what happens on ride day don't we.... Woke early, a friendly insect had kindly bitten me yesterday so leg was itching and on fire. Looked out of the window and didn't see much as the mist was at 2 feet from ground level. Not much if any wind so thankful for small mercies. Tom and Charlotte are moving in next week so the social distancing thing

goes out the window. So, as Lola's normal doggy hotel is still closed Charlotte will try and work from mine. Good luck Charlotte, Lola won't leave you alone. Struggle to get going, in fact takes about 20 miles to warm up. Familiar with the route from the Wolves trip I knew there were plenty of climbs ahead. Radio Sheffield had been in touch yesterday asking if they interview me at 8.45am. I did point out I may struggle for a signal but would stop then for 10 minutes. So 8.40am comes and I have no signal so I nail it until I reach a quarry. Hardly any signal at all. A lovely girl came out of an office asking if I would like to use their phone. When I explained I was waiting for a call she suggested going up a slag heap for a signal. Guess what, they didn't call. Got back going and reached Ashbourne in good time where I met my pal Alex, who was driving my car. Just as I arrived Radio Sheffield called, apologised and put me straight through to the Presenter, nothing like been put on the spot. The mist and moist air

took a while to lift.

Was finally feeling strong. Met Paul at Rudgely and he cycled the last 20 with me. Really was gutted cycling the last few miles. Especially as the route took me past the 'away' pub. Now that would have been brilliant. Arrived at the ground, couldn't get anywhere near the main stand so just had a picture taken outside the away end. Then quickly bike on car and drove home. Weird, very weird. First time that I'd had my kids and their partners in the house since lockdown. Well they are all moving back in with me so I can't say no I guess. It was really nice to get back and see Lola. Charlotte was still working and in a video meeting. I walked past looking like a knackered tramp and waved at her Colleagues.

After a few beers my legs didn't ache. The game began. It must be so bloody hard for the players this. Injuries to Jack O'Connell and Flecky pissed me off. This was put out on social media in the morning by a so called fan. Why would you do that? The game was as I expected.

This season has seen some shit VAR decisions go against us but what I have just witnessed genuinely makes you

think that the powers that be don't
want us in Europe over Man U.
Ollie Norwoods free kick had their
keeper back pedalling and then as he
retained his balance bumped into a
defender and stumbled back a pace.
A goal, for fucksake that was a goal.
The ref was tapping his wrist as if
saying the beep didn't go off. For Christ
sake man surely you could have seen it
went over the line. The keeper literally
held the ball against the inside of
the post. VAR didn't change anything.
We were livid. Poor Lola wondered
what had got into me. Obviously she's
not seen me watch the Blades.
How when we waited 10 minutes to
have Didsy's goal ruled out at Spurs
cos Lundstram didn't cut his toenails
could that have not been ruled out?
Seriously for a money making
machine like the Premier League
to let that happen is just
madness of the highest order.
The excuses from Hawkeye and the
Premier League were a joke. Not a
brilliant performance but we all know it
was 1-0 but as per we were robbed.
There's pretty much a match or two
on everyday. At least the scheduling
gave us till the Sunday to face

Newcastle. Strange one this, I've done this one albeit in two phases but done nevertheless. So it was Sunday at home. After a nightmare day with a defective new laptop I settled down thinking, no worries the Blades will make my day improve. Mmmm how wrong I was. First 10 mins we started well and felt at ease but once Egan had been booked for nothing (I personally have my views why) it was all downhill. After his second yellow it was a nightmare. It seemed like our players had suddenly become colour blind as we just kept passing to the stripes of a different colour. I thought I'd grown out of been in a mood after a shit showing but obviously not.

After a couple of beers I did put it all into perspective and realised what a brilliant season it's been no matter what. Although, some fellow Blades on twitter went into meltdown. I guess these guys weren't about during the later Porterfield and Billy McEwan days. Now that was shit. Remember going to Shrewsbury on a Tuesday night and losing 2-0. It was that bad there were about 20 of us playing cards on the terrace. A few issues now in terms of injuries and suspensions ahead of the trip to Old Trafford. O Connell out, Egan out, Deano can't play. Argh well, you never know. The forecast is for a hot day so will get off early.

Blades struggle with the new normal in big restart at Villa

James Shield
james.shield@jpimedia.co.uk
@JamesShield1

Earlier in the morning, three gunmetal grey and silver coaches snaked out of the car park at Bramall Lane and began ferrying the folk on board towards the motorway.

Their destination was Birmingham. The passengers' – Sheffield United's players, management and coaches who, just under two hours later, arrived at Aston Villa for the first Premier League contest of the Covid-19 era.

Ninety six days had passed since the decision was taken to suspend the fixture calendar. The balls are still round and the pitches still green.

But when United disembarked – swabbed, sanitised and temperature checked – they discovered pretty much everything else had changed.

Rather than preparing in the changing rooms below the cavernous main stand, Chris Wilder and his team were directed towards the media suite in order to comply with social distancing rules.

Pre-match hugs were kept to a minimum and as squad members preferred to swap fist bumps.

Lys Mousset and Tyrone Mings bump fists at the end of the first game back

United did enter a huddle 30 seconds or so before kick-off, though. Some old habits, even in the middle of a health crisis, are going to be difficult to break.

With a minute's silence for Covid-19 victims and taking a knee for Black Lives Matter before kick off, football, post coronavirus, proved to be a strange experience. And a slightly debilitating one too.

Certainly for United who, as the action unfolded in front of four largely empty stands, initially struggled to achieve the same levels of intensity which had seen them climb to seventh in the table, and onto the cusp of the Champions League qualification positions, before sport entered lockdown.

Fighting for survival at the other end of the rankings, Villa appeared to find the silence liberating instead. Indeed, until a hugely controversial moment during the dying embers of the opening period, they had fashioned the greater chances. Or half chances to be exact.

"There wasn't too much quality out there," United's midfielder Oliver Norwood said.

"It was a pretty strange to be honest, with no crowd being in-side the ground, but we're going to have to get used to that."

The incident which enraged United came just before the interval. Orjan Nyland, selected to keep goal for Villa ahead of Pepe Reina and Jed Steer, clearly carried the ball into the back of his own net after collecting an Oliver Norwood centre.

As Billy Sharp wheeled away in celebration and McBurnie punched the air, it suddenly became apparent that play had restarted and the score remained deadlocked. The inquest was still continuing as the two sides towards the tunnel.

By the time they emerged again, for a second half which developed in much the same vein as the first, it had been confirmed a serious technological flaw had cost United dear.

"I couldn't see but all the lads were telling me it was in," Norwood said. "So I was asking the ref why it hadn't been given and he told me his watch or whatever it is they use hadn't buzzed.

"The reaction of everyone out there told you everything you needed to know.

"It wasn't given. It should have been. To be honest, I can't quite believe it but we've just got to take it on the chin."

On the face of it, given the circumstances surrounding the contest and the long break in competition, United would usually have been satisfied with the point which moves them to within four of fourth-placed Chelsea with nine games remaining.

Villa, desperate to preserve their top-flight status following a challenging start to the campaign, were always likely to prove tenacious and highly motivated opposition.

Indeed, Wilder had warned beforehand that, despite looking routine on paper, this assignment would actually prove to be one of his squad's trickiest of the season.

The match officials did not receive a signal to the watch nor the earpiece as per 'Goal Decision System' protocol.

Already he had factored the absence of Jack O'Connell and John Fleck into his calculations ahead of kick-off – electing not to tell the media the duo had been injured during training – he reckoned without what Hawkeye, the architects of the system designed to judge if balls have crossed the goal line, later acknowledged was a terrible error.

"During the first-half of the Aston Villa versus Sheffield United match at Villa Park, there was a goal line incident where the ball was carried over the line by the Aston Villa goalkeeper," a company statement acknowledged.

"The seven cameras located in the stands around the goal area were significantly occluded by the goalkeeper, defender and goalpost. This level of occlusion has never been seen before in over 9,000 matches that the Hawkeye goal line technology system has been in operation."

"The system was tested and proved functional prior to the start of the match in accordance with the IFAB Laws of the Game and confirmed as working by the match officials," the statement added.

"The system has remained functional throughout. Hawkeye apologises unreservedly to the Premier League, Sheffield United and everyone affected by this incident."

A resigned smile crept across Norwood's face when he was informed of the admission. He revealed he had accepted an apology from referee Michael Oliver – "Fair play to him, it wasn't his fault" – but seemed less inclined to accept one from the company boffins.

"There's not much I can probably say without getting into trouble," he said. "All the money in the game, you'd think that wouldn't happen. You wouldn't think technology would be robbing us of three points.

"To be honest, I didn't think we were great and we didn't produce our usual quality. But if we'd have gone on front at that point, I think it might have been different."

Billy Sharp claims a goal as Villa goalkeeper Orjan Nyland appears to carry the ball over the line.

Picture: Paul Ellis/PA Wire/NMC Pool

Ollie Norwood tells referee Michael Oliver just how far over the line the ball was. Picture: Carl Recine/AFP/Getty

Journalists are seen inside the stadium social distancing

CHAPTER 17

Man Utd, 24th June

Man Utd get 4 days rest we get 2, just saying.
Set off at 6.45am. Already toasty. Arranged to meet
Colin McFadden at Tideswell. I met Colin through work
years ago so will be good to see him again.

Amazed how many cars and cyclists are out this morning. The climb up through Stoney Middleton got the legs warmed up for sure. Colin has driven from north Leeds so would have probably set off earlier. Alex (driving my car) was also going to meet us at Tideswell, mmmm although he drove to mine to get my car but realised he had forgotten the key. I said we would meet at Chapel. Yesterday Radio Sheffield had called to say they wanted me on again so I mentioned to the guys we should stop top side of Whaley Bridge so we don't lose a signal. Well we had to stop in any event as the road was closed. The guy on the barriers was a bit of a jobs worth. As we waited I mentioned to him what I was doing and handed him a card which

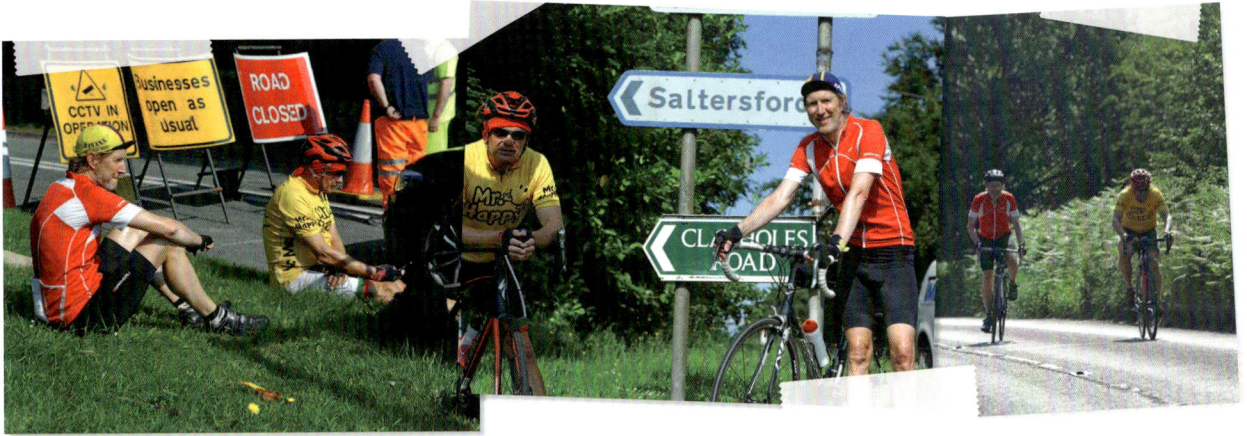

is totally branded with the Children's Hospital logos and colours. When he read it I kid you not he threw it on the floor and mumbled 'not fucking looking at that wi that team on it' turns out he's a pig. I did mention I was doing it for the children's hospital not united but he just mumbled something again, what a prick. After speaking with Toby Foster we followed the diversion up a 10%er. Then down again to literally to 200 yards from where we met Mr Prick. Still all good training.

The weather is gorgeous, people commenting how hot it must be but to be honest it was perfect.

As we approached the tunnels which supported Manchester Airports runways I had a real nostalgia moment. Used to come as kids to see the planes. As we entered the first tunnel I've never felt anything like it. The temperature must have dropped 25 degrees in a second. Weird feeling like pouring hot chocolate sauce over ice cream. Wasn't long till we pulled in outside Old Trafford. What a real shame the 3,000 Blades won't be here tonight. New, weird times indeed.

Stewards were hovering like wasps, can't stand them either, so we took the quick photos then said my goodbyes to Colin and got going. Crazy that I'd cycled to Manchester and was back home by 1.30pm. After the poor showing at Newcastle and a few main men missing it was the first time this season that I actually knew we were going to get a drubbing. Think that's a first under Chris Wilder and not anyones fault. More to do with how well we've done all season. First goal after 6mins, Jesus a long night ahead. We were so far away from where we've been. 3 games back now and not one shot on target.

Paul Tierney. Mention that name to
any Blade over the next few years
and expect to be sworn at.
The Blades first home game back after
Lockdown saw us welcome the gymnastic
team from Arsenal. I personally have no
issue with 2 disallowed goals but the
constant falling over by Arsenal players
cos they were breathed on was a joke
and Tierney got sucked in every time.
It's getting to the point where I'm ready to
walk away from the game. A combination of
the refs knowing fuck all about football and
the powers that be somehow getting their
own way to get their beloved top teams in
the semis and top 4 of the Prem is beyond
a joke. O and guess who was in charge
of the VAR when we played at Villa....
Just sat watching Brighton v Man U. Man
U just scored 2nd goal, no VAR even though
ball went out for throw and they had Shaw
offside....seriously getting close to walking
away from the game. To top it off there
wasn't a mention about either at halftime.
A Thursday evening home game v Spurs and
ongoing injuries with O'Connell still out and
Fleck and Lunny also sidelined. We were all
lifted with the improved performance against
Arsenal in the cup but this was going to
be tough with missing key men. However,
it wasn't long before the beer was flowing

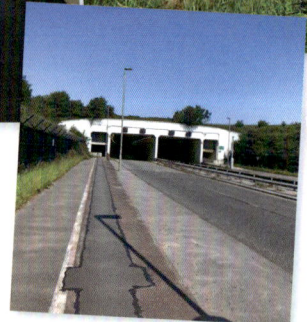

following Berges first goal. The boy is improving rapidly. A few minutes later the mood lowered when Kane equalised. Wait, hang on, really? VAR ruled it out. How on earth was that handball? It's getting stupid now but we will take it as Karma for the stupid decision we had go against us at their place. 3-1 winners and in the circumstances the best performance of the season. I love football again, what a fickle twat I am. We play Burnley on Sunday, KO 12 noon. Why o why did I make the decision to do it on the day? The forecast looks horrendous and I'm gonna have to set off at crazy o clock.

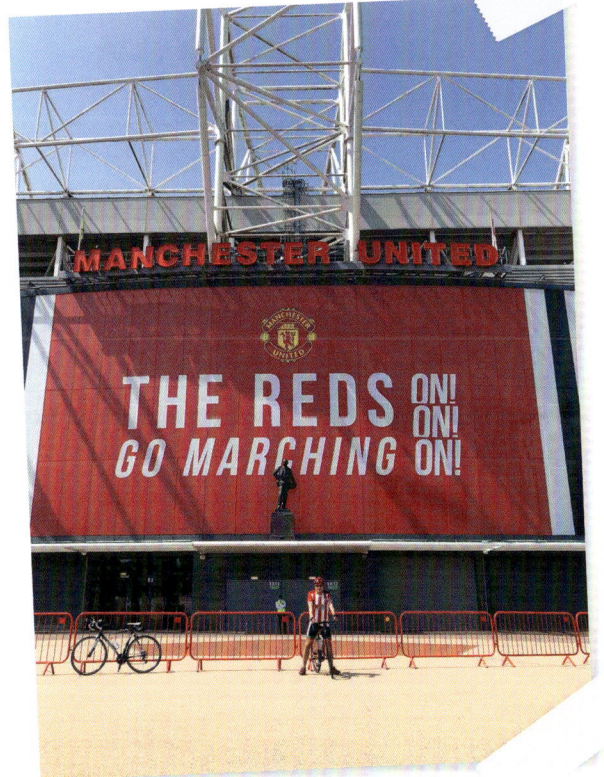

United robbed of their rhythm as Red Devil Martial runs riot

James Shield
james.shield@jpimedia.co.uk
@JamesShield1

At the bottom of the Stretford End, which is usually swarming with over 14,000 people, a banner was draped across one block of empty red seats.

"Football is nothing without fans," it read, quoting the late, great Sir Matt Busby, who ruled over this stadium for nearly a quarter-of-a-century.

Few would care to argue. Least of all Sheffield United, as 'Project Restart' continues to prove a dispiriting experience.

On a sweltering hot evening, inside an empty Old Trafford, where every word the players uttered was clearly audible, an Anthony Martial hat-trick condemned Chris Wilder's side to their second 3-0 defeat in as many outings.

Of even greater concern to the United manager, however, will be the fact his squad remains without a goal since competition resumed following the Covid-19 pandemic.

Now eighth in the Premier League table, the three month break appears to have robbed them of the rhythm, swagger and sheer joie-de-vivre which previously made them such a dangerous proposition for even the division's most powerful clubs.

Bizarrely, United had actually looked the more dangerous of the two sides until the hosts' ability on the counter attack paid dividends in the seventh minute.

United were more enterprising and focused than during either last week's draw at Aston Villa or Sunday's loss to Newcastle.

And the Blades tested the Red Devils' mettle on several occasions before eventually falling behind when Martial reacted quicker to Marcus Rashford's cross than Chris Basham.

Deputising for the ineligible Dean Henderson, Simon Moore should have been picking the ball out of the back of his net again soon after when Martial turned provider for Rashford, only for the England striker to inexplicably shoot wide from point blank range.

Although Manchester United continued to probe a rearguard also missing Jack O'Connell and John Egan, Ole Gunnar Solskjaer's men did not have things entirely their own way – despite David de Gea remaining untroubled between the posts until substitute Oli McBurnie tried his luck from range in the 83rd minute.

The only trouble was, Martial had already pounced for the second and third time by then.

He converted Aaron Wann-Bissaka's cross seconds before the interval and then, with 16 minutes remaining, applying the finishing touches to an intricate move crafted by Bruno Fernandes and Paul Pogba.

TEAMS

■ **Manchester United:** De Gea, Lindelof, Maguire, Pogba (Pereira 80), Martial (Ighalo 80), Rashford (James 80), Fernandes (McTominay 80), Shaw, Greenwood (Mata 80), Wan-Bissaka, Matic. Not used: Romero, Bailey, Fred, Williams.

■ **Sheffield United:** Moore, Baldock, Stevens, Robinson, Jagielka, Basham, Norwood (Berge 46), Fleck, Lundstram, McGoldrick (Zivkovic 65), Mousset (McBurnie 46). Not used: Verrips, L Freeman, Sharp, K Freeman, Osborn, Rodwell.

■ **Referee:** Anthony Taylor (Cheshire).

Anthony Martial celebrates scoring his hat-trick. Picture: Michael Steele/NMC Pool/PA Wire.

'Toxic playing' means Wilder's men have 'fallen off a cliff' say fans

Here is what Blades fans on Twitter thought of last night's result and performance at Old Trafford.

@tyronej1984: Absolutely fell off a cliff since the restart. We look done. Desperately need to show something resembling our usual selves in the final seven league games. #twitterblades #SUFC

@Hstew97: What am I watching here, just get the season over with and regroup for next season. Toxic playing like this and it's a shame to see with all the hard work they've put in all season #SUFC #twitterblades

@TravelingBlade: Thank Christ that's over. Started off promising, ended up depressing. #MUNSHU #sufc #twitterblades

@LiamJamesC: Full faith in Wilder to get it sorted, but frankly, not good enough. Again. No fight in any of the three games since the restart, players letting Wilder down in my opinion. #SUFC #TwitterBlades

@mike_g_sheff: We go again against @Arsenal on Sunday. Chin up Blades #sufc #twitterblades #MUNSHU

@Glavesys: Don't worry blades fans. When we win FA cup we get in Europe anyway #twitterblades #sufc

@LewisBagshaw: Do we know that football is back? Anyone told the team? #sufc #twitterblades

@Blades_Mad: Of course Man United have multi-millions of pounds worth of talent, and that certainly is a major advantage. Of course. I think the effects of the last two performances before this one still linger. Taking today in isolation, we've had worse results #sufc #twitterblades #MUNSHU

@Pazzamore1: It's June 2019, someone says "Blades will be eighth with seven games left and in the FA Cup quarter final this time next year". You would have laughed. Let's all just remember that. #sufc #twitterblades

@The_Bladesman: Thought our performance in the first half was good. Second half the intensity and effort went out of the window. We're fighting for European places. Why does it look like we don't care?

@ryanmathews1893: We lack strength in depth. We've been lucky with injuries until now JOC, Fleck, Moose. We need players who can come straight into the team and fill the void. Forget the starting 11, we need players on the bench who can impact a game #sufc #twitterblades

@MartyKBlade: Could be worse, could be Norwich, Villa, Bournemouth... #sufc #twitterblades

Tired Blades left chasing shadows and their form

James Shield
james.shield@jpimedia.co.uk
@JamesShield1

This, Chris Wilder reminded beforehand, was the catchweight contest to end all catchweights contests.

In one corner stood Manchester United – serial trophy winners, lavish spenders and the Premier League's most efficient money making machine.

And then, peering suspiciously at them across Old Trafford's perfectly manicured pitch, was Sheffield United – a team which viewed trips to Bradford and Bolton as highlights of the season before climbing out English football's third tier three years ago.

The match was like pitting Kell Brook against Tyson Fury. Or asking a "Ford Fiesta" to outrun a "Ferrari" as Wilder had preferred to put it 48 hours earlier.

A meeting between two clubs with absolutely nothing in common apart from their sporting surname.

A glance at the table, however, brought one of boxing's favourite maxims to mind. With only two points between them at kick-off, the size of the dog doesn't settle fights. It's the size of the fight in the dog.

The Blades had no shortage of desire during a swelteringly hot evening.

But what they lacked was the attention to detail and searing turn of pace required to prompt a change of tactics from the Norwegian. Lys Mousset, presumably introduced to provide exactly that, failed to reappear for the start of the second-half after succumbing to injury.

"The goals we conceded were ridiculously cheap," Wilder said, after watching Anthony Martial hit all three.

"I'm not interested in excuses. They were basic errors. You see the moment and the ability the players up top have got here and so you've got to defend at your best.

"So to keep giving the ball away, and to defend in that manner, is very disappointing."

Travelling to the North-West with a squad depleted by injury, suspension and in the case of Dean Henderson, rules prohibiting on-loan players from facing their parent clubs, it suited Wilder to peddle his 'David versus Goliath' narrative and tell anyone who cared to listen, following Sunday's defeat by Newcastle, that United were "on the ropes." Privately, though, you suspect he didn't believe a word.

United are at their best, Wilder knows better than anyone, when they're written off, disregarded and told they've just accepted an impossible mission.

The only trouble was, shorn of some of their most influential performers, that's what their latest assignment became when Martial claimed his second just before the interval.

"Even in an empty stadium, you need a foothold in the game," Wilder continued.

"To concede after seven minutes, it puts us on the back foot. If you keep conceding possession to quality players then you're going to get hurt.

"We thought 'Let's get in at 1-0 down' because it could have been worse and we're still in it. So we concede a minute before half-time.

"From our point of view, we've got a lot to look at."

Unbeaten in six before the Covid-19 pandemic brought competition grinding to a halt in March, United have struggled to rediscover their trademark rhythm and momentum since returning to action.

After controversially being forced to settle for a draw at Aston Villa – where a Hawkeye and VAR inspired omnishambles denied Oliver Norwood a winning goal – they looked a pale shadow of their usual selves en route to another 3-0 loss at St James' Park.

The break has suited some top-flight sides. United are not among them. Nor, given the fact they unashamedly wear their hearts on their sleeves, do they look particularly comfortable inside empty stadia.

Once so creative, they have averaged only one shot on target per game over the course of the last three outings. In these conditions, matches become tests of pure ability alone rather than ability allied with emotion.

"We looked pretty tired out there, which I suppose is understandable when you are chasing around after the ball," Wilder said.

"Whether it's back to basics or whatever, we've got to find an answer pretty quickly because I don't want us to fall off a cliff."

"In the end, it turned into a difficult night for our football club and a pretty easy one for them," Wilder added.

Bookended by strikes from Martial, the first half proved a dispiriting experience for United.

The second was a stroll for the hosts.

The Frenchman's opener came when he reacted faster than Chris Basham to Marcus Rashford's cross.

The second will also have been far too simple for Wilder's liking – with Martial, now enjoying his most profitable season in English football, again getting in front of a defender to meet Aaron Wann-Bissaka's centre.

From that moment on, as you would expect, the fixture became something of a walk in the park for Solskjaer's men. Bruno Fernandes and Paul Pogba, who impressed alongside the Portuguese, pinged the ball around in front of a United midfield which lost Norwood during the interval.

With Mousset hobbling and Richairo Zivkovic not introduced until just after the hour, Manchester United also felt comfortable effectively playing with four men in attack and continuing to press high upfield.

As United toiled and inevitably tired, it was no surprise to see them concede a third with Martial completing his first career hat-trick after combining with Pogba and Fernandes.

It was also the first league hat-trick scored by a Manchester United player since 2013.

John Lundstram shoots wide as Paul Pogba of Manchester United looks on. Photo: Michael Steele/Getty

Anthony Martial gets away from Sander Berge and Chris Basham

Solskjær: 'We should have scored more goals'

Ole Gunnar Solskjær says his Manchester United side "could and should have scored more goals" in the first half of their comfortable victory over Sheffield United at Old Trafford last night.

The Blades made a more assured start than in either of their two games prior to this clash, but were rocked when Anthony Martial scored two in the first half, theb completed his hat-trick in the second.

And Solskjær said afterwards: "At times it was very, very good football.

"We could and should have scored more goals to put the game to bed before half-time.

"It's always worrying when you go in at half-time knowing that's the case," the manager added.

"But I was really pleased with the way we pressed and stopped Sheffield United from playing.

"We did what we did and made it difficult for them to get out.

"But there is still more to come and we shouldn't be 100 per cent happy with it."

Bruno Fernandes, Solskjær's £67 million midfielder, was excellent after being paired in midfield with Paul Pogba, making his first start since September.

"I thought we controlled the game," Solskjær continued.

"Paul and Bruno showed some quality and it's exciting for us to be working with talent like this.

"Paul is still a bit away from his best form.

"That's natural because it's his first start since September. He's been working hard.

"Now it is a case of keep on working, onto the next one."

Ole Gunnar Solskjær with Chris Wilder after the match

CHAPTER 18

Burnley, 5th July

Weird dreams, wind waking me all night then alarm goes at 3.30am. Jesus this is going to be a twat.

It's still dark as I clip into the pedals. After a mile it's 4am and I see a guy walking, well swaying (and not because of the wind) obviously on his way home. The wind is horrendous and I'm really worried this can be done. On the way to Owler Bar I feel I'm on a treadmill as I don't feel I'm moving. Anna and Jordan will be bringing me home and we worked back from kick off which is 12 that I need to be at Burnley by 10. The wind drops a little as I drop into Hathersage. Going past Ladybower at 5am I'm amazed at how many cars are parked up. Maybe doggers. The climb up the Snake Pass isn't too bad but when I reach summit o my god I have never experienced wind like it. The descent to Glossop is normally worth the climb but not today. I was shitting myself. I went all the way down with one foot out the pedal. My forearm was in agony when I reached Glossop. Colin was meeting me at 7.15am but I was there by 6.45 so suggested meeting at Stalybridge. It was good to ride the last 30 with Colin. Although there were so many long climbs. The last long descent was no reward as the brakes were on due to the wind. Nice to speak to the stewards outside the ground, felt normal. Said farewells to Colin then set off back. Need to be back before kick off. Just after setting off we saw the Blades coaches, how weird is that, coaches. Made it back just in time for Kick off. So I will have to sit stinking for another 45 minutes.

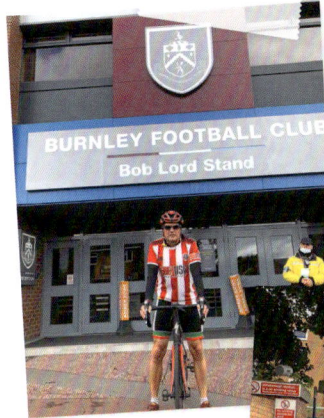

Happy with performance. Tough team Burnley and to come away with a point is great 3 days after beating Spurs. Two proper managers who are honest and won't stand for diving about. We move on. Hopefully my promise re Champions league away games is now safe. The visit of Wolves 3 days later and another changed team due to an injury to Didsy. So we now have Fleck, Lunny & Didsy out the starting 11. However the performance was fantastic. Deano hardly had a save to make. All saying how we would take a point when Egan AGAIN and from a corner (we never score from corners) scored with a minute to play. The lounge erupted, imagine if we were at the Lane, 30,000 would have gone bananas. Despite the obvious ongoing Covid worries what a time to be a Blade.

A young Wednesday fan, Shay is doing his own Triathlon raising money for BlueBell Wood Children's Hospice and starting by cycling between S6 and S2. His dad got in touch so I was delighted to cycle down and meet him at 'their' place. What a lovely lad and Dad. Cycled with him to the Lane. It reminds me that banter and rivalry is ok but does have a ceiling. Maybe one day Shay will cycle to all Wednesday's away games.

The visit of Chelsea brought optimism after such good showings against Spurs and Wolves. What a performance! To make it even better David McGoldrick scores his first two of the season. Still not getting the respect we deserve as it's always the opposition that have off days. Souness continually calls us Sheffield. We were the original United ffs.

Wilder happy with a point as Egan rescues 'leggy' Blades

James Shield
james.shield@jpimedia.co.uk
@JamesShield1

Supposedly, you always get what you pay for. Anyone who follows football, however, knows that isn't always strictly true.

The game is littered with folk who can burn through money quicker than it takes Chris Wilder to sink a Peroni after beating Tottenham Hotspur and players who cost a king's ransom but who deliver pounds, shillings and pence. So is it strictly true that Sheffield United and Burnley, who drew 1-1 at Turf Moor, are two clubs who punch above their weight?

In financial terms, the answer is yes. Neither Wilder nor Sean Dyche have access to the same type of funding as others inside the Premier League's top 10.

But while anyone can spend, only the intelligent can spend wisely. And patrolling the technical area in front of The Bob Lord Stand were two managers who, in terms of nous and savvy, are comfortably in the black.

Moments before kick-off, an audio clip of Dyche outlining his sporting principles boomed out from the stadium's public address system - which had still been cranked up to eleven even though there was only a smattering of people inside.

"People talk about old fashioned values," he said, in those immediately recognisable gruff tones. "But those values, well, they've actually been more modern." Wilder, who was striding purposefully across the pitch when the tape started playing, could be seen nodding his head in agreement. In fact, so similar are their outlooks, he probably wished he'd scripted them himself.

Despite the obvious differences in terms of their tactical approach, Wilder and Dyche both subscribe to the theory that the team always, absolutely always, must come first. Players are selected and signed on their ability to improve the group as a whole rather than attract lucrative sponsorship deals or sell replica shirts. And above all else, they need to be willing to roll up their sleeves and work.

"I was delighted to get something out of it," Wilder said, after John Egan's second-half effort cancelled out James Tarkowski's opener for Burnley. "I thought we looked a little bit leggy at times, which perhaps is understandable, and so bits of our usual quality wasn't there.

"But we kept on going, kept on fighting and in the end took something home with us. So well done to the boys."

Wilder had made no secret of his admiration for Dyche and the manner in which Burnley have built their infrastructure during his eight years in charge. Indeed, speaking on the eve of this fixture, he described the hosts as the perfect template for United to follow as they look to establish themselves in the top-flight after being promoted last term.

So deep is the respect which exists between the two men, it was no surprise to see them locked deep in conversation throughout the warm-ups. But when the action got underway, they barely acknowledged one another. Wilder and Dyche might be friends, They are also fierce competitors.

United had been creative and clinical during Thursday's win over Spurs so, with Jack O'Connell named on the bench following injury, it was no surprise to see Wilder select an unchanged starting eleven in the hope of inspiring an equally effective performance. It was a ploy which worked in part, with United finding themselves trailing at the interval only because they failed to convert any of the numerous openings forged against one of the best defences in the competition. Had Oli McBurnie's first minute shot not been scrambled away by Nick Pope or Jack Robinson's foot stayed on the right side of the line when he launched a Howitzer of a throw-in towards Sander Berge, who tapped home at the far post, then the poor piece of marking which allowed Tarkowski to slide home following Dwight McNeil's set piece would have been a minor irritation rather than the defining moment of the half.

"To come away with a result, from a losing position is always pleasing," Wilder acknowledged. "But, to be honest, I was a little bit disappointed that we found ourselves chasing it because we shouldn't really have been behind. We should have been up in the game."

Deam Henderson was powerless to prevent Tarkowski sliding home from close range when Jay Rodriguez flicked on McNeil's delivery just before the break. But he excelled himself with only minutes remaining when, after Egan's emphatic volley, he tipped an Erik Pieters shot around the post as United's admirable determination to keep on forcing the issue presented Burnley with an opening.

Wth United continuing to probe and enjoying the better of the possession without applying serious pressure on Burnley, Wilder began tweaking with United's personnel and shape. O'Connell was introduced, making his first appearance since competition resumed last month, alongside captain Billy Sharp. Lys Mousset was thrust into action shortly after.

But it was Egan, scoring the first Premier Premier League goal of his career, who finally prised apart a rearguard which had entered the match searching for its third successive clean sheet when he pounced on Sharp's flick following a short corner routine.

Burnley: Pope, Taylor, Tarlowski, Brownhill, McNeil, Westwood, Rodriguez, Pieters (Gudmundsson 95), Bardsley, Vydra (Wood 65), Long. Not used: Peacock-Farrell, Brady, Thompson, Dunne, Thomas, Benson, Goodridge.

Sheffield United: Henderson, Baldock, Stevens, Basham (Rodwell 75), Egan, Robinson (O'Connell 54), Norwood (Sharp 54), Osborn, Berge, McGoldrick, McBurnie (Mousset 66). Not used: Moore, Jagielka, K Freeman, Zivkovic.

Referee: Peter Bankes (Merseyside).

John Egan celebrates scoring for United at Turf Moor. Photo: Clive Brunskill/NMC Pool/PA Wire

Sean Dyche shakes hands with Chris Wilder after the match

Egan strikes to score for the Blades and rescue a point at Turf Moor

David McGoldrick and Josh Brownhill battle for the ball

CHAPTER 19

Leicester, 16th July

Feel low, very low.
Lola needs two ops on both rear legs so next
few months aren't going to be easy at all.

Set off at 8.30am, very reasonable.
Within no time I'm near East Midlands
airport. Anna & Jordan are meeting me
at the ground at 3pm so I either need
to slow down or they need to set off.
Go through a road blocked sign
and a guy shouts your can't get
through.' Luckily I could otherwise
I would be going 10 miles back.
Make it into Leicester with no issue.
To say they're in lockdown still,
there's plenty of people about.
In fact by the river there were
about 10 guys on the booze
and it wasn't even 2pm.
The Blades were poor tonight but
again let's be real about it.
Before we get time to draw breath
we're back at the Lane for the last

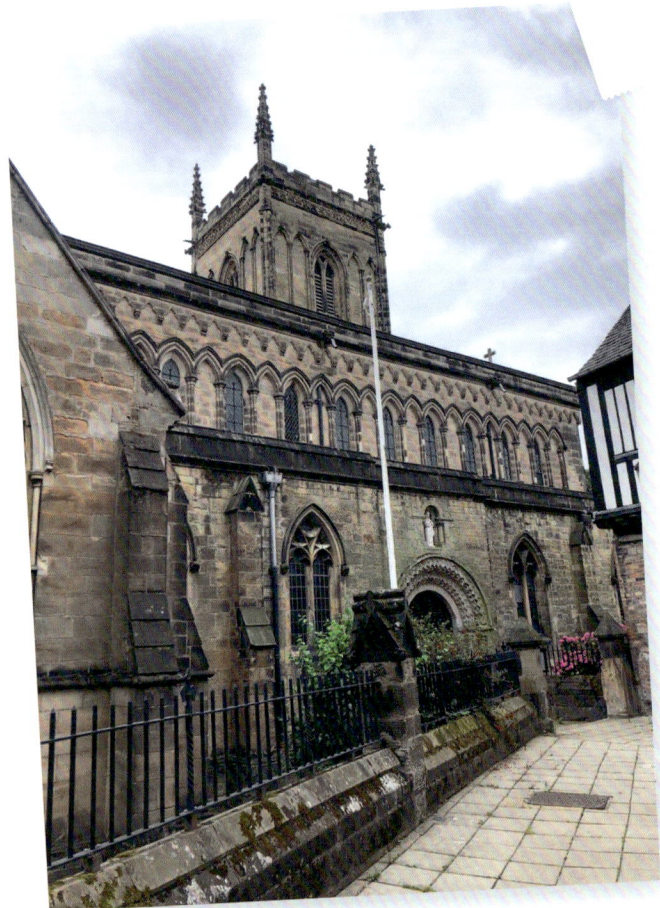

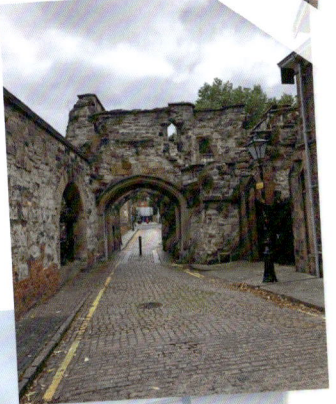

home match of the season v Everton. Was supposed to be my big send off. Dave McCarthy at the Club had kindly sorted it for me to be presented to the fans prior to this match. That was obviously pre the little bug that's been circulating the planet. A frustrating game saw us go down 1-0 and all but ended our European dreams. To be fair I'm more than happy to accept the top half dream.

Wednesday the 22nd July. Have really gone down hill the last couple of weeks, but starting to come round and am looking forward to the last one, Southampton. Off to fetch Paul from his Mums.

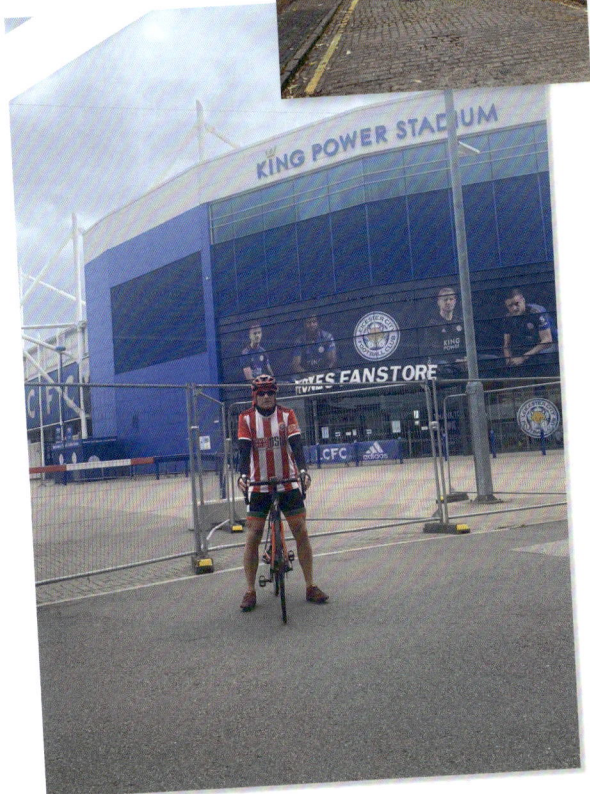

Loss a huge but not fatal blow to lacklustre Blades' hopes

LEICESTER	**2**
UNITED	**0**

James Shield
james.shield@jpimedia.co.uk
@JamesShield1

Just behind the Lineker Stand, the blue, white and brick edifice which greets visitors to the King Power Stadium, sits a nondescript patch of litter-strewn weeds.

It was there, before Leicester City moved into their shiny new purpose built home nearly 20 years ago, where Sheffield United enjoyed one of the greatest days in their history.

They sealed promotion to the old First Division following a 5-2 win on that now un-loved patch of waste ground – or Filbert Street as it used to be known.

That match, and the people who took part in it, are assured of their place in Bramall Lane folklore. But their successors, managed by a veteran of Dave Bassett's legendary team, last night returned to the city intent on achieving something much bigger – delivering a place in Europe.

Chris Wilder, the person responsible for turning a side supposedly destined for relegation into serious contenders, has spent most of the past four months discovering in-novative new ways of talking down their chances and dodging questions about the possibility.

So much so that, before Premier League football emerged from the shadow of coronavirus, one suspected a career in politics might beckon when he finally waves goodbye to the dug-out.

Although this result dealt a blow to United's hopes of reaching the continent next term, it was not a fatal one.

City, who saw Ayoze Perez and substitute Demarai Gray score either side of the interval, are now assured of entry into at least the Europa League.

United remain eighth but only a couple of points behind sixth-placed Wolves - not that Wilder was in any mood to acknowledge as much afterwards.

"We've taken some huge steps forward over the last year or so, I thought we took one back out there tonight," he said.

United's 36th assignment of the season proved to be a test of Wilder's tactical nous, having decided his men lacked the intensity to drag themselves back in following Perez's opener.

Brendan Rodgers paid the visitors the compliment of changing the Foxes' approach and, with Jamie Vardy and Harvey Barnes both reaping the benefits, could well be tempted to persevere as he attempts to nail down a place inside the top four.

Across the technical area, Wilder spent much of the evening deep in conversation with his assistant Alan Knill. United changed personnel. They changed shape. But, try as they might, they failed to change the flow of the contest with substitute Gray stretching City's lead during the closing stages.

United had made a positive start, with David McGoldrick sweeping the ball over the crossbar after Oliver Norwood sent George Baldock scampering through. But it was tough going from that moment on.

United travelled to the East Midlands knowing that a win – followed by ones of Everton and Southampton – would see them qualify for the EL regardless of results elsewhere.

But ever since climbing out of the second tier, this is a squad which has punched consistently above its weight.

The match, however, proved to be a sobering experience.

City, ditching their usual possession based game and electing to turn United instead, caused the visitors all manner of problems with their positioning and pace.

Wilder, probably encouraged by the fact only Perez had scored, delivered his verdict in the shape of a triple half-time substitution. It did not have the desired effect and, when Gray deservedly stretched City's advantage, he provided another.

"Their fight was better than ours," Wilder said. "I think that's the best way of putting it."

Ben Osborn had expressed concerns beforehand that John Fleck's return to fitness following injury would bring to an end his run in the starting eleven. The midfielder has been one of Wilder's most influential performers over the past few weeks.

Despite naming Fleck as his own player of the year ahead of kick-off, Osborn deservedly retained his place.

But he spent the majority of the first-half chasing opponents and making blocks as City emerged as the dominant force of the first-half. Fleck was introduced thereafter.

The hosts' movement and precision had already caused United problems by the time Perez pounced in the 30th minute. The Spaniard had already gone close, heading wide at the far post, before calculating his angles perfectly and threading a low drive past Henderson's outstretched palm.

Nineteen year old Luke Thomas, the third youngest player to make their full Premier League debut for City, provided the assist.

Although O'Connell and John Egan both went close

inside the hosts' penalty area, the second-half continued in much the same vein as the first as the pace of Barnes and Vardy continued to cause problems.

Indeed, were it not for the brilliance of Henderson, Barnes would surely have joined Perez on the scoresheet after the interval.

Twice the 22-year-old found himself bearing down on goal and twice Henderson came to United's rescue with his feet.

Youri Tielemans sliced wide following Barnes' second effort.

But Henderson was powerless to prevent Gray doubling City's lead in the 79th minute – the former Birmingham City

attacker drilling an angled shot just inside the far post soon after being introduced.

TEAMS

■ **Leicester:** Schmeichel, Justin, Morgan, Evans, Tielemans, Vardy, Barnes (Gray 77), Perez (Choudhury 71), Ndidi, Bennett, Thomas. Not used: Ward, Iheanacho, James, Mendy, Praet, Johnson, Hirst.

■ **United:** Henderson, Basham (Sharp 59), Egan, O'Connell, Stevens, Baldock, Norwood, Osborn (Fleck 46), Berge (Lundstram 46), McGoldrick (Mousset 46), McBurnie. Not used: Moore, Jagielka, K Freeman, Robinson, Zivkovic.

Referee: Michael Oliver (Northumberland).

Dean Henderson punches clear to keep the scoreline down. Photo: Cath Ivill//AP/Getty

Chris Wilder shakes hands with Jamie Vardy after the match. Photo: Getty

Player ratings

HENDERSON 8
Made a good early stop with his legs to deny Vardy and then did well to deny Perez. A couple more saves from Barnes kept it at 1-0 in the second half.

BALDOCK 6
Good awareness in the opening minutes to pull the ball back for early McGoldrick chance.

BASHAM 6
Produced a typically energetic performance. Went off for Sharp in second half

EGAN 5
Caught in possession over the halfway line in the lead up to Leicester's second goal, as the Blades chased a way back into the game

O'CONNELL 6
Tested Schmeichel for the first time in the game in the second half, with a deflection goalwards from Egan's header

STEVENS 6
Not his finest of games down the left wing, although he was far from alone

NORWOOD 6
Superb early ball set Baldock free in behind the Leicester defence. Some of his passing early on was very good. Lost it a bit as Blades chased the game

OSBORN 5
Couldn't grab the game by the scruff of the neck and was replaced by Fleck at half time

BERGE 5
Couldn't get to grips with the game. Was replaced at the break by Lundstram

MCBURNIE 6
Evans had the better of him.

MCGOLDRICK 5
Came close early on but didn't have his usual influence on the game. Went off at half-time

MOUSSET 6
Gave attack a different dimension when he came on at half time

FLECK 6
Looked understandably rusty.

LUNDSTRAM 5
Gave a bit of extra in energy in midfield.

SHARP 6
Replaced Basham, put a few threatening balls into the box.

Demarai Gray celebrates scoring the Foxes' second goal. Photo: David Davies/AP/Getty

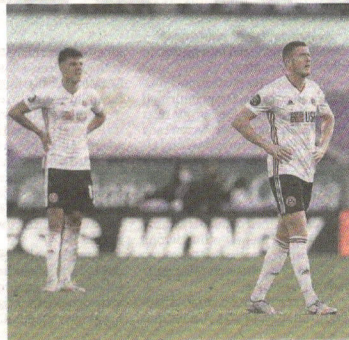

United players react after conceding the second goal. Photo: Getty

David McGoldrick came close to scoring. Photo: AFP/Getty

CHAPTER 20

Southampton, 26th July

Paul very kindly had offered to do back up and camp with me.
Didn't sleep that well and was up early.
Fast start in fact fast most of the day. Paul's sense of direction
I found out after 40 miles was about as good as my Dads. In
fact at one point I thought my car could be on eBay.

Wayne and Paul were, in their own way very supportive, with their whatsapp comments. Such as, Paul 'my right calf is beginning to hurt' Wayne 'he doesn't know he's born, all this in and out the car is exhausting'. When I complained about the head wind Paul's reply was 'yeah when I feel the headwind I turn the air con off'. Great lunch at a familiar spot and off again. Was concerned I was too quick and knew I would pay for it but when you feel it you wanna burn it up. The wall started building with 20 miles left and wow those bricklayers were quick. Was really struggling with 15 to go. Managed to amble home, now to get the tent up. Found out there was a nice boozer 30

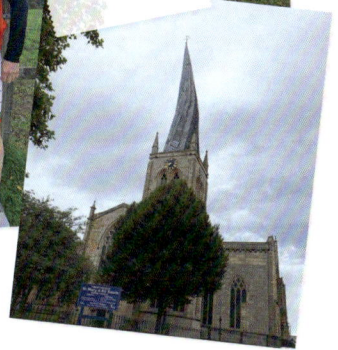

minute walk down the canal path. Wow. Some very interesting people. A guy growing his own weed, a family moved over from Chicago. So good to chat to different people. The pub was unreal. A real gem. They had the social distancing lark off to a tee. Brilliant. I asked Paul who he thought the killer was (as it was so much like Midsomer). First night in a tent for a few years and had a restless night. A rather annoying crow seemed to be having a row with a Wood Pigeon which wasn't ideal. Packed up very efficiently and in no time I was off. 7.30am start so made good progress. Stopped at Witney, a lovely Town I've stopped at before. Never thought my accent was that strong but a lady on the next table asked 'are you from Sheffield?' Turns out she's from Stocksbridge and a Blade. Make it to Radcott and my usual visit to the Swan which is adjacent to Thames. Gorgeous place. Last few miles are ridiculously tough but felt strongish. The camp site has a shower thank goodness. Felt so much better to be clean. A friend I met watching the Blades drove to meet Paul and I for the evening. Another lovely pub in Lambourn. Got chatting with the doorman. A giant of a man who mentioned he's an actor so I pushed him to give us some 'works of art' cracking fella.

Slept like a baby. Woke early packed away, got told off by lady who runs site for pitching tent in the wrong place, even though her husband watched us do it. This is it. 58 miles to go.

Just want to get it done. The route was beautiful again. I need to be careful to stay within myself. Had arranged to meet a fellow Blade, Steve who lives in Chandlers Ford. It's not often you're cycling 250 miles from home and a guy cycles past saying 'Hey James'. Good to ride in with Steve, especially as he knew the local shortcuts. The gentleman that Steve obviously is slowed and let me ride solo the last few yards. I looked to my right and saw the steel of the ground above me. I put my foot down at the same time as a single tear rolled down my cheek. What started as a promise 5 years ago has just been completed I saw four familiar people walking towards me, Paul, Sarah, Rowan and Jude. Sarah had driven across from Gloucester to see me finish. It was all very brief. Felt incredibly flat, up until March I had been dreaming about arriving and falling into the arms of 3,000 Blades. Just wanted to get home. Felt guilty that I didn't stay and have lunch with Sarah and the boys. Receive some incredibly nice comments

via social media. Get in the car and drive home. The rain was something else. At one point I was driving at 20mph on the A34. As we got closer to home I stuck some old Whitesnake on and Paul and I were shouting the lyrics, badly, for the rest of the journey. Say farewell at his Mums then straight home and straight into the Miners Arms where 5 years earlier I walked in after getting back from Gillingham......

A week later I cycle to BDTBL and meet Lucy from The Children's Hospital. They want to present the 'big cheque' not keen but happy to get young Max involved. Max was treated in the Hospital for Cancer and is thankfully clear now. There just there is why I'm proud to have helped such a fantastic cause. Sarah, his Mum, must have been to hell and back. Mum, Dad, Anna, Tom, Charlotte, Jordan and my cycle buddy Alex are also there. I look around and a security guy hands me a signed away shirt which the club kindly donated so I can auction. Really proud to have helped raise £16,500 to help the poorly children but feel so flat that the Blades family aren't here. When will we sing loud and proud again?

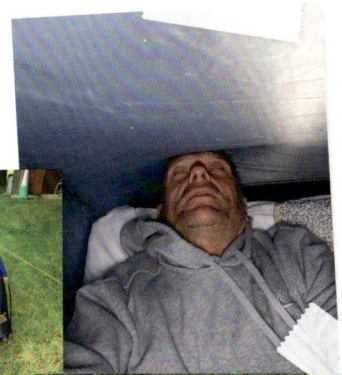

Wilder reflects on campaign after defeat to Southampton

John Lundstram celebrates his goal with Sander Berge. Photo: Andrew Boyers/Getty

SOUTHAMPTON 3
UNITED 1

James Shield
james.shield@jpimedia.co.uk
@JamesShield1

Ryan Bertrand booted the ball, referee Peter Bankes blew his whistle and that, as they say, was that.

Three hundred and fifty one days, 14 wins, 12 draws, 12 defeats and one global pandemic since taking their first not so tentative step back into the Premier League, Sheffield United signed-off a memorable season for all sorts of different reasons.

But mostly, Chris Wilder reflected following this visit to Southampton, because of the achievements of his players and the progress they have made.

"This is probably the strongest division in Europe and possibly the strongest division in the world," he said, after United finished ninth in the table despite this 3-1 defeat at St Mary's Stadium.

"And we've come where we've come, facing clubs who are absolute giants. The lads have represented our club absolutely brilliantly."

The outcome of the match will be a source of frustration – Che Adams scoring twice

The Blades congratulate Lundstram after he opened the scoring.

against his former club and Danny Ings netting once after John Lundstram had earlier broken the deadlock.

But United will look back upon their work over the past 11 months with an immense amount of pride.

Nearly a year ago, a little over 30 miles to the west, Wilder's men were being told that relegation beckoned when they prepared to begin the new top-flight campaign against AFC Bournemouth.

Eddie Howe's men have gone down but Wilder's charges have flown. Despite being told they were too unsophisticated, too naive and simply too inexperienced to survive let alone prosper in such exclusive company after 12 long years away.

"The players have given me everything, absolutely everything, but of course we also need to move forward," Wilder commented.

"We've got to move forward because that's what everyone else will be doing. And I'll be doing my absolute utmost to make sure that happens.

"I'll be doing everything I can to make sure we keep heading in the right direction and getting better at everything we do."

With the transfer window swinging back open in less than 24 hours time, United had travelled south with one eye on the Saints and the other on their recruitment plans.

The opening exchanges revealed where Wilder will look to improve before September. And why, having named a short-handed bench following injuries to Jack O'Connell and David McGoldrick, United found themselves chasing the ball for the first 15 minutes, but still created the best early opening.

Unfortunately it was spurned, with Billy Sharp prodding the ball straight at Alex McCarthy after being released by Lundstram.

The United captain – a former Southampton player – appeared to be caught in two minds as Oli McBurnie charged forward in hot pursuit, screaming for a pass and making Sharp aware of his presence.

Wilder, who concedes his squad must become more clinical and calculating in order to build upon their progress of the past 11 months, shrugged his shoulders and turned away.

But his dismay turned to delight midway through the first-half when Lundstram powered home from close range. Receiving possession from John Fleck, Enda Stevens' cross slipped through Jannick Vestergaard's legs after being shielded by Sharp and reached the midfielder – who converted from close range.

Lundstram thought he had extended United's advantage soon after but his thumping effort was saved by McCarthy.

"The game is always decided in both boxes and that's what happened here," Wilder said, tracing how the contest eventually slipped from United's grasp.

"They were clinical in our area. We weren't clinical in their area. But there were some tired minds and bodies out there."

Lundstram's impact on the first-half – impressing both in and out of possession before claiming his fifth of the campaign – underlined the midfielder's importance to a United side who showed great discipline in the face of Southampton's constant probing.

But with contract negotiations between him and the club seemingly making little progress, doubts must remain over Lundstram's long-term future at Bramall Lane.

Wilder, who would prefer the player and his agent to accept United's offer and allow everyone to move on, also faces an anxious wait before discovering if Dean Henderson will return next term.

The goalkeeper, on loan from Manchester United, has been superb since first arriving in South Yorkshire two summers ago. If this was his last appearance in a United jersey, it actually turned out to be a pretty disappointing one.

Henderson looking crestfallen when Adams' shot flew past him at the near post early in the second period. For all their slick exchanges and movement, Southampton's equaliser was created in pretty scrappy circumstances; the ball falling kindly for the former United youngster following a challenge by Sander Berge.

Adams has matured beyond all recognition since leaving United soon after Wilder's appointment in 2016.

He was sold to Birmingham City as part of the fundraising exercise which helped construct the squad which later delivered the League One title.

He showcased his instincts once again with a little over a quarter-of-an-hour remaining – sweeping the ball beyond Henderson, who was powerless to intervene, after Kyle Walker-Peters' shot had cannoned into a defender.

Ings added the third from the spot after being clipped by John Egan as substitute Oliver Norwood attempted to shepherd him across the area.

"I actually think that was a game we should have won in the first half," Wilder said. "We should have been out of sight at the break."

Player ratings

HENDERSON 6
Looked disappointed with himself after Adams scored his first goal at his near post.

BALDOCK 7
Played the full game, meaning he has played every minute in the Premier League for the Blades this season.

BASHAM 6
Showed good defensive instincts to block from Ward-Prowse after Egan's attempted clearance ended up fortuitously in his path.

EGAN 7
Took the captain's armband when Sharp went off and can be proud of his achievements this season.

J ROBINSON 7
A superb defensive challenge prevented Adams from testing Henderson from 10 yards out.

STEVENS 6
Picked up an assist after his underhit cross wasn't dealt with and Lundstram scored.

BERGE 6
Used his stature to good effect at times.

LUNDSTRAM 7
Superb ball down the line set up brilliant chance for Sharp, put the Blades ahead and later forced a superb save from McCarthy.

FLECK 6
Industrious without the ball and inventive with it. Set up a chance for Stevens.

MCBURNIE 6
Involved in a good move that almost led to Lundstram scoring. Replaced early in the second half by Zivkovic

SHARP 6
Had a great chance to open the scoring on his return to St Mary's. Then missed another golden opportunity before going off.

ZIVKOVIC 6
Replaced Sharp but didn't do anything that cried out 'sign me'.

CLARKE 6
Another brilliant servant for the Blades, rewarded for his goals over the years with a final Premier League appearance.

NORWOOD N/A
Came on for Basham with Blades chasing the game and gave away the penalty.

Richairo Zivkovic closes in on Nathan Redmond. Photo: Glyn Kirk//Getty

Oliver McBurnie turns away from Jannik Vestergaard.

George Baldock has played every minute of Premier League season

There were many Sheffield United heroes during the club's first season back up in the Premier League.

Chris Wilder, obviously, and Alan Knill. The players, too, with special mention reserved for Chris Basham, not only United's longest servant in the squad but also a hugely popular choice as Player of the Year.

One man who probably won't recognise he falls into the same category is the author of this book. But what James Kemp did during the 2019-20 season was every bit as heroic as those stirring deeds on the pitch that took United to a ninth place finish.

To cycle to all 19 away league games (and a Cup tie!) in the name of such a worthy cause as Sheffield Children's Hospital was as gutsy and noble an act as any by a Blade, not least because the final six of those trips were undertaken despite there being no chance of James watching United in action due to Covid-19.

That his endeavours raised £17,500 was hugely deserved and I hope it made all those aching limbs worthwhile.

By the time I caught up with James outside the Emirates in January, he had already travelled 1,800 miles and climbed the equivalent of two Mount Everests.

Just listening to the tale of his travels made me gulp. I'd moaned en route to the win at Brighton & Hove Albion before Christmas about being diverted due to flooding on the train track between London and the south coast.

But I quickly realised, on chatting to the man dubbed 'Blade-on-a-Bike' by fellow supporters, I'd had no right to whinge at all. Not after hearing what James had endured on his ride south from Dronfield while also suffering from a nasty bout of man-flu.

Learning what a lift he'd had one morning, having woken up feeling very down, from all the messages on social media from fellow fans made me realise just what a big emotional toll undertaking something like this must have.

It was why, after the interview had appeared on The Athletic, I was so pleased to see the comments from our readers. 'What a guy!', 'Brilliant story and man' and 'I'm guessing he doesn't eat too many greasy chip butties on the way?' were joined by plenty of promises to donate to the fundraising effort.

Worthy recognition of a brilliant effort by 'Blade-on-a-bike'.

- Richard Sutcliffe,
The Athletic

I had a go at this long-distance cycling lark. And until Blade on a bike James told me about some of his two-wheel adventures, I was quite proud of my 90-mile dash from North Derbyshire to Boston, Lincolnshire. In three days.

I had the pleasure of being able to plan just about every detail; I picked the most flat-as-a-pancake route from my front door that I could find, I checked out the weather forecast before setting out in the middle of summer and I was able to amble along tracks and lanes which were well away from busy roads.

It would hardly have counted as a training run for James.

Embarking on his latest adventure, he didn't enjoy such luxuries. When the Premier League released its 2019/20 fixtures, he studied them with excitement and trepidation before checking out his maps and accommodation guides. However, his plans had to change big style almost immediately when TV companies annoyingly began to reschedule most of Sheffield United's match days and kick-off times.

He realised that nothing on the fixture list, and therefore his personal calendar for the next nine months (or so he thought), was set in stone.

James clocked off the miles as United chalked up the points. I met up with him outside West Ham United's London Stadium after he had survived a most gruelling ride through strong winds and driving rain. It had been tough enough travelling there by car.

The arrival of a pandemic called a sudden halt to his odyssey - ironically, at a time when it seemed that just about everyone else in the country was taking up cycling.

Then, when football returned, not only did James get back in the saddle, but he had an almighty number of journeys to complete in a short space of time. And to add to the unpredictable nature of his year, although he had concerns over cycling in our summer weather, it was cold and not heat which nearly killed him in July!

So although the Blades narrowly missed out on qualification for Europe in 2019/20, it was certainly a Champions League performance from their man in the saddle. And I know readers of our magazines were left in awe at his exploits.

- Mike Firth, editor,
Heron Publications

Acknowledgements

To the hundreds of people who encouraged and donated to such a worthy cause I thank you.

My daughter, Anna and her Fiancé, Jordan who have not only helped with back up when they could but were there when my lights were dimmed.

Also Anna for helping me with Social Media, well it is her job!

To my Son Tom and his girlfriend Charlotte who have babysat my furry baby, Lola

My Mum and Dad for being there, always.

To Radio Sheffield, The Sheffield Star, John Shires and Calendar, Look North, Alan Biggs & Richard Sutcliffe (The Athletic) who all helped me get the word out there.

To a truly brilliant lady at BDTBL. I will keep her identity secret, but she knows who she is.

To Luke Prest for giving up his free time to design the excellent front cover illustration.

To all the wonderful people I met along the 3,000 miles you have restored my faith in Humanity, thank you.